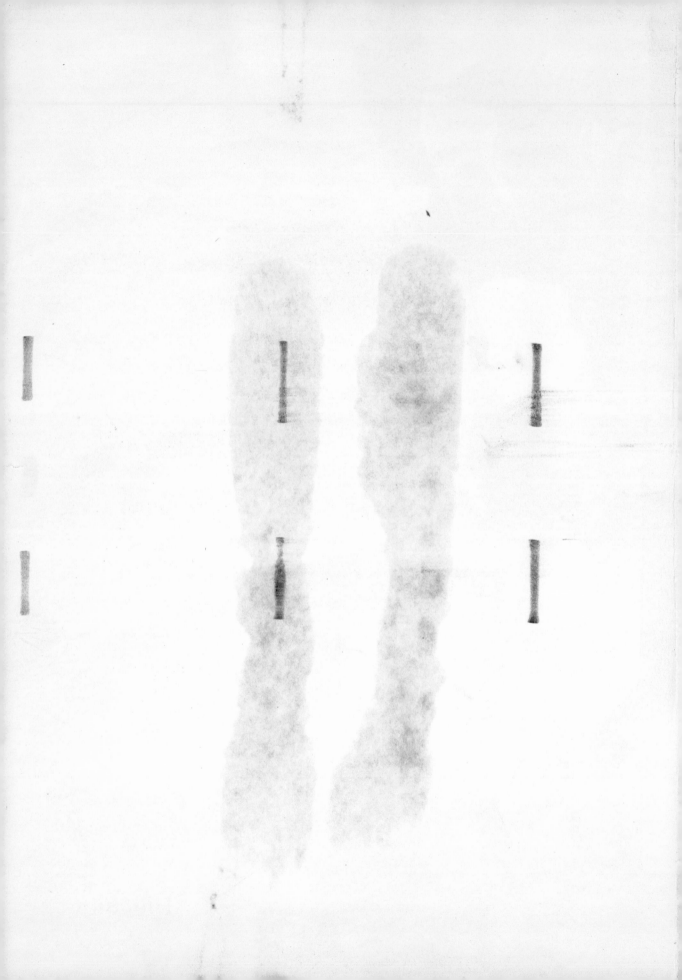

The Wonderful World of Archaeology

The Wonderful World of

Archaeology

Ronald Jessup

Doubleday and Company Inc.

Garden City, New York.

Library of Congress Catalog Card Number 68-14675

Copyright © 1968 by Aldus Books Limited

Copyright 1956 by Rathbone Books Limited (Adprint Limited)

Printed in Yugoslavia

Contents

Certain words and phrases in this book are followed by the symbol ☞. Whenever you see this symbol it means that you can look up the word or phrase in the alphabetical glossary at the end of the book and find more information or a fuller definition of the term.

1   The Past Sets a Problem

Amid the broad expanse of Salisbury Plain, in the west of England, rises a great circle of standing stones called Stonehenge☞. Who built it? How long ago? What was its purpose? Its builders left no written answers to these questions and for many years people were content to guess. In the Middle Ages writers told fantastic stories of its being moved bodily from Ireland by Merlin, the wizard of Arthurian legend, to serve as a British memorial to warriors killed by the Saxons. During the 17th and 18th centuries various people thought that it was a Druids' temple, an astronomical observatory, a memorial to the Celtic warrior-queen Boadicea, or even, perhaps, the work of the Phoenicians☞.

Not until the 19th and 20th centuries did archaeologists seriously look in order to learn the facts. Even some 40 years ago, when more than half the site had already been excavated, the origin and purpose of this remarkable monument were still a mystery.

Since then methods have improved, new scientific techniques have been introduced, and more work has been done on the site. Today, thanks to our new knowledge of radioactivity, we are able to say that the first phase of this impressive building operation probably began between 1900 and 1700 B.C. We also know that some of the stone blocks were transported from southwest Wales, nearly 150 miles away. We can picture how Stonehenge looked before it fell into ruins. But there is still much to learn.

This is just one example of the kind of problem that the past has set. The bits and pieces of evidence from which such problems can be solved are sometimes scattered over a wide area, often buried in the soil. The task of finding them, recognizing them, and fitting them together like the pieces of a jigsaw puzzle, to make a clear and meaningful picture, is the special task of archaeology.

Let us look at part of the history of one small corner of the world so that we can begin to see how the archaeologist sets to work.

One of the mysterious 300-year-old statues on Easter Island in the Pacific.

Above, the circle of Stonehenge. Right an Etruscan earring, 600-500 B.C.

About 800 B.C., before Rome had risen to greatness, the fine Etruscan civilization appeared suddenly in the northwest of Italy. Where did the Etruscans☞ come from? What kind of people were they? How did they live?

Unlike the builders of Stonehenge they left many writings: some on tombstones, some on cups and vases, and one, strangely enough, preserved in the bindings of an Egyptian mummy☞. Yet these writings are of less help than we might at first suppose. Although the Etruscans used the same alphabet as the Greeks, they used it to make quite different words, and so far only a few score of them have been translated. Further, many Etruscan inscriptions consist of little more than proper names. Some day an inscription may be found that is repeated in Etruscan and some known language, such as Greek. If so, it will give us a key.

Meanwhile the archaeologist depends on other ways of probing the mystery of this great, vanished civilization. He finds a vase or a gold trinket here, a bronze statuette or a piece of gay and lively wall painting there, and from a careful study of many such objects, most of them of great beauty and fine workmanship, he gradually builds up a picture of the men and women who made and used them. He learns something of their art and religion, of their quest for food, of the shape and condition of their houses and settlements, of how they fought, how they worked, how they spent their leisure.

With the help of photographs taken from the air, he reveals the obliterated sites of long-forgotten roads, and thus learns something of

the Etruscans' ability as engineers and organizers. By finding and recognizing objects of Etruscan workmanship in other parts of the world, he has learned that this ancient people probably traded with places as far apart as North Africa and Asia Minor.

The archaeologist may also learn something from the works of the classical authors. But here, as in ·the legend of Horatius holding the bridge single-handed against Etruscan troops, it is often hard to sift fact from fancy.

Writers of classical times believed that the Etruscans came from Asia Minor, and there is certainly evidence to support that belief. Their religious ceremonies and some of their earliest art show a close likeness to those of certain eastern Mediterranean lands, and the fact that their first settlements were near the coast indicates that they may have arrived by sea. Some authorities, however, still believe that these people were natives of Italy.

Yet, in spite of some remaining doubts and differences of opinion, archaeologists are well on the way to fitting together the pieces in this corner of the puzzle of the past.

How did the past become a puzzle? How have the pieces been lost or buried? It has happened in many different ways, but few are more dramatic than the burial of Pompeii.

This fine Roman city was overwhelmed completely in A.D. 79 by the disastrous eruption of the volcano Vesuvius. The historian Pliny the

Younger, whose famous uncle witnessed the beginning of the disaster and was finally killed in it, describes how the city was buried deep in a rain of ashes and windborne lava. Many of its inhabitants met their death while fleeing from the terror; others were suffocated in the cellars to which they had run for shelter. Private houses, public buildings, factories, and workshops—all were engulfed. But not everything was destroyed; the lava that covered the city also preserved much of what it buried.

The lost Pompeii was first rediscovered more than 300 years ago—not by archaeologists but by engineers. While digging an underground canal through the soft lava, they uncovered several inscriptions and many houses with walls of brightly painted plaster. There was further digging during the 18th century; then in 1860 a systematic plan of work was adopted: quarter by quarter and house by house the town was methodically examined.

Today we can see much of the ancient city of Pompeii almost as its long-dead inhabitants saw it. Here are the ovens and mills of a bakery, there a tavern with its pots, hanging lamp, and petty cash still in place. Here, again, is preserved the figure of a boy blinded by ashes as, with a little food in a basket, he tried to escape.

We see that in Pompeii, a town of busy commerce and trade, the public buildings are large and impressive. Here are fine places of entertainment, a great amphitheatre☞ for staging events out-of-doors, and splendid public baths. But it is the simple messages found scratched or painted on the walls that make the ruins of Pompeii so appealing and so at one with our own time: advertisements of all kinds, election slogans, business notes, love notes, shopkeepers' tallies, children's first lessons.

The very calamity that brought death and destruction to the city has, in a sense, made it live on to the present day.

Nature has several other ways of burying and thus preserving the past. Most of them are not as sudden as that which engulfed Pompeii, but often they are just as effective.

The dry sands of Egypt overwhelmed the royal tombs in the Valley of the Kings☞: writings thus preserved on fragile papyrus provide knowledge of the early Egyptians, Greeks, and Romans that otherwise would have been lost. In Central Asia, valuable discoveries concerning bygone times have been made in the sand-covered rubbish heaps of a settlement abandoned nearly two thousand years ago. At Skara Brae, in the Orkney Islands, off the north of Scotland, blown sand covered the stone houses of a Neolithic (New Stone Age) village; about a hundred years ago a violent storm uncovered it, intact.

Over the long centuries, land surfaces rise and fall. By the sinking of land in the Alpine regions of Europe, once-flourishing lake-side and lake-island settlements of prehistoric peoples slowly became covered by

Top, at Pompeii, a statue of the god Apollo stands poised to shoot an arrow.
Lower, part of a mosaic shows how Pompeiians liked to decorate their villas.

11

water and by natural deposits of peat. When, a century ago, an exceptionally dry, cold winter caused lake and river levels to drop, the frames of wooden houses once again came into view, complete with structural details. Not only the houses were revealed, but also examples of food, tools, weapons, wooden utensils, baskets, and even textiles. From such evidence, many details of life in Neolithic and Bronze-Age Europe have been learned. We now know, for instance, that Bronze-Age men enjoyed apples and pears, and sprinkled poppy seed on their bread.

Climate itself is an important factor in the breaking up of the past. Nowhere is this more apparent than in regions of extreme heat and constant heavy rains, where vegetation grows rapidly. Many old cities of Southeast Asia, among them Angkor Thom, with the nearby temple, Angkor Wat☞, are buried deep in tropical jungles. The deserted Mayan cities of Middle America, too, fell century by century into further decay until at last they were covered by a protective mantle of the very jungle that had caused their ruin.

In the other extreme of climate, frozen silts slowly covered the remains of prehistoric man and the now extinct animals—such as the mammoth—that he once hunted for food. Miners in Alaska and men digging for buried mammoth ivory in Siberia often unearth such remains. From them the archaeologist learns more not only about early man's hunting weapons, but also about his migrations from continent to continent.

Timbers found in dried-up lakes help us to picture a prehistoric lake village.

In addition to Nature, man himself has been responsible for breaking up and burying the material remains of the past. In times of peace, men have often used the stones of ancient monuments to build new houses. In times of war, towns may be devastated and never rebuilt: the Hindu fights with the Muslim invader, and his cities fall and lie desolate for seven centuries right down to our own time.

In Roman London a great fire lays waste much of the settlement about the River Walbrook: houses collapse into ruins, the rubble of old foundations is leveled up, life begins afresh, and new houses are built on the site. The river floods, breaks its course, and forms a quagmire. Long after, people of the Middle Ages live and work in the same place, and human settlement continues through peace and war, fire and flood, down to the present day. The ground level has risen continuously until there are now 30 feet of accumulated human history below London's streets.

Man has also broken up the pattern of the past in his roles of collector, hoarder, and robber. Valuable antiquities have been moved from place to place at the whim of travelers in search of souvenirs; the Romans buried the silver of earlier times against the coming of the barbarian invaders; and what more might we now know of the ancient Egyptians had there been no robbers to steal from the treasure-laden tombs of the pharaohs!

A Roman bronze and a first-century B.C. shield found in the Thames at London.

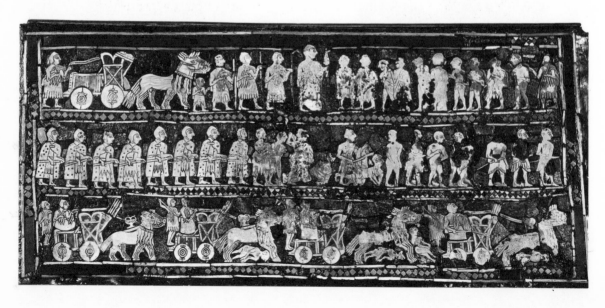

2 Preserving the Clues

When the things of the past are buried by nature or destroyed by man, the memory of them may easily be lost. But man, like nature, can preserve as well as destroy. In words and in pictures he can capture the living incidents of his own time and leave them on record for future generations.

In ancient Egypt and Mesopotamia, men often left inscriptions☞ on the walls of temples and palaces, recording the circumstances in which they were built; artists and craftsmen also made vivid records of the daily life around them. One famous mosaic from Mesopotamia, the "Royal Standard of Ur," clearly pictures the life of a prince, in peace and war, five thousand years ago. But ancient Mesopotamia not only produced recorders of current events; it also produced antiquaries.

Some 40 years ago, while excavating at Ur☞, where history lies buried layer under layer, Sir Leonard Woolley made a remarkable discovery. On the floor of a room built about 550 B.C. for the use of Princess Bel-Shalti-Nannar, sister of the Babylonian ruler Belshazzar, he found objects dating back to 1400 B.C., 2000 B.C., and 2280 B.C. How could these things have strayed from older layers, near the bottom of the excavation, to the highest and most recent level? Fortunately Woolley found the answer. Nearby was a drum-shaped clay tablet bearing copies of very ancient inscriptions, together with an original inscription made only a century or so before the time of the Princess. The last one explained how the earlier inscriptions had been found and copied out "for the marvel of beholders." It was, in fact, one of the world's earliest museum labels; the room itself was a museum, and Bel-Shalti-Nannar was a collector of antiquities.

Her father, King Nabonidus, shared her love of the past. In repairing Ur's great Ziggurat☞, or "Hill of Heaven," he carefully noted that the original building was erected by a much earlier king, Ur-Nammu. He expressed pleasure at finding a foundation tablet in an ancient temple.

The Standard of Ur records the reign of a prince about 1600 B.C. One side shows the luxury of his court, while the other suggests the strength of his army.

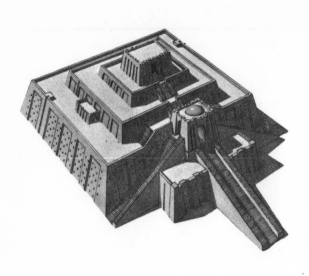

Left, the ziggurat as Ur-Nammu built it; right, helmeted Sumerian soldiers.

In Egypt, too, there were kings with similar tastes. About 700 B.C., King Shabaka ordered that the writings on a worm-eaten document, already 2000 years old, should be copied in stone. A century later, under King Psammetichos, many statues were carved in styles of far earlier times—evidence of a lively antiquarian interest.

The greatest of all antiquaries of long ago was Herodotus, born of a well-to-do family at Halicarnassus, in Asia Minor, in the fifth century B.C. Perhaps his love of the past was inspired by reading the old heroic stories of the Iliad and the Odyssey.

As a young man he traveled widely in western Greece, Asia Minor, and Syria, visiting many of the places that figured in those stories. Later he saw lands that were the homes of earlier civilizations: Egypt, Mesopotamia, and the northern coast of the Black Sea. He visited famous cities such as Babylon, Tyre, and Ecbatana, capital of the Medes. He saw the great pyramids, and was acquainted with many prophecies of the Oracle of Delphi.

On his journeys he seized every opportunity of learning all he could about the history and people of the places he passed through. Often he stayed for some time, making careful notes from first-hand observations, recording conversations, measuring old monuments, enquiring about the people who built them, and about anything else that engaged his inquisitive mind. Herodotus was once described as "the father of lies," but he was in fact an accurate reporter of what he saw and heard.

The impression of a Babylonian cylinder seal of the first millennium B.C.

Eventually, the fruits of his work and travels were embodied in a long book that began with these words: "This is the History of Herodotus of Halicarnassus, published in order that what has happened may not be forgotten of men by the passing of time. . . ." Then, against a background of the history of Persia, the lands it had conquered, and its wars with Greece, Herodotus set down all he had seen and heard.

The result was a history of the greater part of the then-known world. Not only did he describe the people themselves, their work and play, their customs and their legends, but also the geography of their countries, with especial reference to antiquities. In his own lifetime, his writings were made known to a wide audience by means of public readings. Today, his *History* is often regarded as the first great prose work in European literature, and Herodotus himself as the father of archaeology. (The word archaeology comes from two Greek words that together mean discussion of the past.) In original and in translation, his famous work has been passed down from generation to generation, and is still read with interest and enjoyment. But not all written history of this period shared the same fortune.

In 331 B.C., a century after the death of Herodotus, the fine city of Alexandria, named after Alexander the Great, was founded on the Mediterranean coast of Egypt. It very soon became not only a busy trading port, but also a unique storehouse of learning. Ships of many lands brought merchandise to its warehouses, scholars from far and wide studied in, and added to, its vast library. At its height, this famous library contained no less than 700,000 scrolls. Had they survived to our own time they would have added immeasurably to our knowledge of the past. But in 145 B.C. riots and civil war destroyed a great part of the library. The destruction was completed about 47 B.C., when a Roman force under Julius Caesar set fire to the nearby Egyptian fleet. A new library later arose and amassed a smaller collection of scrolls, but, centuries after, these too suffered a similar fate. Thus, part of the history of the civilizations of Greek and Roman times, formerly preserved in writing, was lost.

Some four centuries after Alexandria fell to the power of Rome, the mighty Roman Empire itself began to totter. It was already diminished in size, split politically into an eastern and a western half, and economically into several self-sufficient units, and hard pressed by dissatisfied non-Roman troops inside its own borders. Now Rome's western regions fell a surprisingly easy prey to the onslaught of invading barbarians.

At its height, the Empire of Rome, stretching from the Atlantic Ocean to the Persian Gulf and from Scotland to the south of Egypt, had given men a sense of belonging to a large, closely knit world. Its long, unbroken history, reaching back through time to the last glories of ancient Greece, Persia, and Egypt, had also built up among the peoples of Europe and the Near East a strong sense of oneness with the past.

When the Western Roman Empire fell, the peoples of Europe, both east and west, soon lost the old sense of unity. The Byzantine part of the

A copy of an ancient Greek painting shows Alexander pursuing Darius of Persia.

Empire, around Constantinople (now Istanbul), where men were surrounded by so many buildings and monuments of earlier times, kept much of its feeling of being linked to the past. But Western Europe, cut off from the homelands of early civilizations, soon found the link of history weakening.

Yet even there, some memories of antiquity still survived. Late in its history, Imperial Rome had adopted Christianity as its religion, and when Rome fell, the scholars and monks of the Christian Church preserved at least a little of the learning embodied in the works of earlier Greek, Latin, and Hebrew writers. St. Augustine, who lived in North Africa at the time of the sack of Rome, wrote much that helped to keep alive the thought and teaching of the great Greek philosopher, Plato. St. Jerome, the first scholar of his age, who died in A.D. 420, not only translated the Bible into Latin for the first time, but also wrote a book from which many later chroniclers formed their idea of history.

For several centuries, the Bible and the works of a handful of early Christian scholars formed almost the only written sources of Western Europe's knowledge of antiquity. In an age when few people could read and fewer still could write, even that knowledge seldom extended far beyond the walls of monasteries. As the centuries passed, monk after monk wrote and rewrote the story of past times—and, in exactly the same way, drew and redrew maps—with little or no reliable new information to help them. Consequently, they often had to rely upon imagination and tradition to fill the gaps.

Typical medieval Bible illustrations: St. Luke, and Jonah and the whale.

A third-century sculpture depicts armored Romans fighting barbarian invaders.

The maps of the Dark Ages and the Middle Ages that followed, unlike those of ancient Greece, were not intended to set out hard facts about geography; they were rather the means by which the map maker expressed his hopes and fears, his religious beliefs, and his imaginings about a world of which he knew little. In a similar way, the medieval historian, while a careful chronicler of his own times, could seldom set down established facts about the ancient past. Instead, he described what he felt should have been, or what he thought might have been. So few pieces from the true picture of the past remained in Western Europe that men had almost given up the attempt to fit them together.

Without facts to guide them, they painted a new picture of history which, quite unavoidably, owed much to their imagination and bore very little likeness to the reality.

What, we may wonder, did the world look like to the medieval monks whose lovely hand-illuminated manuscripts so often depict such strange and moving combinations of incidents from various books of the Bible?

The Bible gave them, in the form of a simple, vivid story, an account of the world's creation and the beginning of the human race; it also gave them the hope of eternal life when life on earth ended. The Garden of Eden and the Gates of Heaven represented the beginning and end of man's journey through life. That journey, leading to an everlasting future, was man's first business. To the monk of the Middle Ages, the importance of the past lay in the fact that it often carried a message that might help to sustain men on the road.

Many books of the Bible, including Genesis, Exodus, Joshua, and Samuel, told in simple narrative form how nations, tribes, and individual men and women of the past had taken part in the age-old battle between good and evil. By reading such books, scholarly men became familiar with the names of many great cities and countries of old and with the nature of important events of bygone times. They knew the names of Babylon, Nineveh, Tyre, and Sidon; they knew something about the building of the Tower of Babel, the siege of Jerusalem, and the destruction of the walls of Jericho. Their knowledge, it is true, was neither deep nor detailed; but the stories of the Old and New Testaments undoubtedly kept alive a real, though limited, interest in the past and its traditions.

Other stories of early times were also known to the Western World: for instance, the story of the founding of Rome, of the wooden horse of Troy, of Alexander's great conquests, of the threat to sacrifice Iphigenia, Agamemnon's daughter, to propitiate the winds that had left his Greek fleet becalmed and helpless.

But, scattered here and there, were other and more powerful reminders of the past: Roman villas and viaducts, triumphal arches and memorial columns that still remained more or less intact. In Rome, for example, was the magnificent column erected by the Senate to commemorate the Emperor Trajan. With its great spiral of carvings representing Trajan's victories, it must always have been regarded, by the citizens of Rome and the many pilgrims who visited the city, as a historical document in stone.

In 11th-century Britain, monks of St. Albans, seeking stone to repair their fine abbey, found it by excavating on the site of the Roman town of Verulamium, nearby. Their careful record of Roman inscriptions, glass, and pottery shows that they had a lively interest in antiquity. A century or so later, other excavations were made by the monks of Glastonbury. They found human bones and a lead cross inscribed with the name of King Arthur. For centuries afterwards these finds were believed to prove beyond doubt that Arthur, hero of so many British legends, had really lived.

Interest in the past was certainly alive, but it was still limited to the monk and the privileged scholar. Ordinary people had very little share in it until the Crusades—the Holy Wars in which men from all Christian parts of Europe banded together to wrest Jerusalem from the hands of the Muslims.

Slowly the Crusaders reestablished the contacts with the past that their ancestors had lost. The prolonged wars took them to ports that had flourished in Greek and Phoenician times, and to the lands of the Bible stories. Their very castles were sometimes built from the stones of Roman walls. Chroniclers who accompanied them kept journals as they moved from one sacred place to another.

Arab trading ship, and an eighth-century British coin modeled on an Arab dinar.

At the time of the Crusades (roughly A.D. 1100-1300), knowledge of past civilizations was also moving westward in other ways.

The Muslim Empire, reaching from Portugal to Persia, was founded at a time when many of the writings of early Greek scholars were still preserved in eastern Mediterranean lands. Muslim scholars translated Greek writings on astronomy, geography, medicine, and geometry into Arabic, and advanced these studies considerably in their universities. Several of the most famous of the Muslim universities were in Spain, at Cordoba, Salamanca, and other large towns. They attracted many Jewish and a few Christian students from other parts of Western Europe. These students often took back new knowledge to their own countries, thus helping to stimulate a revival of learning.

During the three centuries that followed the close of the Holy Wars, the outlook of Western Europe steadily broadened. Contacts with the East continued to grow. New fruits, spices, precious stones, exotic fashions, richly figured silks, and all kinds of luxuries never before known came by sea from Asia into the ports of Venice and Genoa and moved overland northward and westward. Men learned of other ways of life and other ways of thinking. New arts and crafts began to flourish. European women saw themselves for the first time in glass mirrors.

One of the wall paintings in the ancient Mayan city of Chichen Itza, Mexico.

The learning of the ancients, kept alive through the Dark Ages inside the Muslim Empire, flourished anew and quickened men's desire to know more of the world and its wonders. Seamen, equipped with new navigational instruments and knowing more of astronomy and geography than ever before, were ready and anxious to undertake voyages to find and open up new lands and to discover new sea routes to the Indies.

It was in search of such a sea route that Columbus made the voyage that opened up the Americas. This great turning point in history placed Europe midway between the ancient civilizations of the Old World and the future civilization still to arise in the New. But, from the point of view of man's awareness of the past, it did even more. Only a few years after Columbus first crossed the Atlantic, other travelers began to realize that America itself already had many chapters to add to human history. Buildings of great size, tools of fine workmanship, skillful carvings, all spoke of a long period of development among the native peoples of Middle America.

No wonder that Western men, who had so long lost a clear vision of the past, now began to realize its fascination and to take a keener interest in it than they had ever taken before.

3 Unearthing History

The age that witnessed the opening-up of the New World, often called the Renaissance, was a time of great opportunity and rapid progress. The breakdown of the old feudal system had given men a new freedom of thought and action; printing, which developed faster, perhaps, than any craft previously known, quickly helped to spread new knowledge and bold philosophies; expanding world trade brought opportunities of wealth and leisure to a fast-growing merchant class.

The wealthy landowner of the Middle Ages was often unable to read or write, but the merchant princes of the Renaissance were proud to be counted among men of learning, as patrons of science or the arts. Many, conscious of their debt to antiquity, were beginning to enrich their reading of Greek and Roman history by collecting about them the finest examples of classical art. Thus written history began to take on a new significance.

In the Italian city-state of Florence, when the great Medici family was at the height of its power, the discovery of an ancient manuscript was considered only less important than the acquisition of a province. Cosimo de Medici (1389-1464) ornamented his sumptuous palace with many precious pieces of ancient art, a unique collection of marble statues, pottery, glass vases, gems, coins, and medals. Among the statues that Ferdinand de Medici (1549-1609) assembled at his villa in Rome, one, at least, came from the home of the Roman Emperor Hadrian.

Two hundred years later, gentlemen of means were still keen collectors. It was fashionable for those who could afford it to make a prolonged tour of Europe, as a means of completing their education, and often such men brought back antiquities from Greece and Italy to beautify their homes or their estates. Relics were no longer quite so easily found as they had been when the collection of antiquities began; but men were by now learning to dig for the past and even to search for the remains of ancient buildings within the structure of modern ones.

Roman treasure is still occasionally found by accident. This silver dish of the fourth century was turned up by a plow at Mildenhall, England, in 1942.

In Britain, and in northwest Europe generally, appreciation of classical times showed itself in the building of the great houses, which were commonly modeled on Roman-Italian (Palladian) styles of architecture; in America, particularly in the northeastern states, interest in the past played a part in the naming of such towns as Ithaca, Marathon, Homer, Troy, and Carthage.

Yet interest in bygone times was by no means confined to interest in Greece and Rome. The man who brought back relics from his Grand Tour was becoming equally ready to search for antiquities beneath the soil of his own estate. There was a growing realization that almost every nook and corner of the world held evidence of the vast panorama of man's story.

As yet there was nothing approaching skilled excavation, but people were fast realizing that history was not confined entirely to books. Much of it was buried beneath their feet.

The fashion of studying history in the open air spread; digging for the past became a popular pastime. Digging led to writing and discussion. Many books were published, many antiquarian societies formed. It was not long before the man of wealth and culture ceased to be a mere collector of curios, and became an amateur of archaeology.

Prominent among the antiquarian societies of the 18th century was the Society of Dilettanti, formed in London in 1733 to discuss the Mediterranean journeys of its members and to encourage good taste among collectors of antiquities.

View of the Parthenon, built in the fifth century B.C. *as a temple to Athene.*

Toward the middle of the century, James Stuart, an English artist, and his architect friend Revett spent three years in Athens, copying inscriptions☞, making drawings, and carefully recording the outstanding ancient monuments of the city. Later their work was published by the Dilettanti, and so much interest did it arouse that shortly after its publication the Society decided to send out an Ionic expedition.

This was an important landmark in the history of archaeology—the first organized expedition.

Many other travelers, inspired by this example and after studying the works of classical Greek historians, wrote entertainingly of their own travels in search of the grand and the picturesque in Greece. Collectors of antiquities of all kinds set to work on a really large scale. Outstanding among these was Lord Elgin, who was appointed British Ambassador to Turkey in 1799, at a time when Turkish territory included much of the area that was formerly the homeland of Greek civilization. From the Turkish government he received a permit to remove carved figures from the Parthenon. This temple had been bombarded more than a century earlier, and many such works were still lying on the ground. Under Elgin's direction 200 cases of marble sculptures were collected and sent to England. After some years of neglect they were eventually bought by the British government and today the Elgin Marbles are still a highly valued possession of the British Museum. It was after seeing imported Greek art treasures in London that Keats wrote his famous "Ode on a Grecian Urn."

Part of the frieze of the Parthenon sent to England by Elgin in the 1880s.

A 1700-year-old Roman vase shows Perseus with the head of the Gorgon Medusa.

From 1821 to 1832 the Greeks waged a long War of Independence against the Turks, which resulted in the setting-up of an independent Greek kingdom. Travel and archaeological exploration in Greece now became easier, and soon other countries besides Britain began to send expeditions to Greece and its islands.

By 1829 the French were excavating works of art from the ruins of Olympia, which had played so large a part in Greek sport, religion, and politics. Some ten years later the Germans began work at Delphi, the site of the Oracle of Apollo, below the peaks of Parnassus.

Temples and tombs, public buildings and private houses, all came under the scrutiny of the archaeologists. Towns were cleared of rubbish, shrines and treasuries explored. Marble sculptures of incomparable beauty, such as the Winged Victory of Samothrace, several fine statues of Venus, the Charioteer of Delphi, and the Hermes of Praxiteles, became famous the world over. The everyday life of ancient Greece became known as it had not been for the past 1500 years. Excavation was making it possible to add to, and sometimes even to rewrite, history.

Throughout the 19th century, almost every civilized nation of the world—not least the Greek people themselves—took part in unearthing the dramatic story of this ancient land. Thus Greece, which gave us the father of archaeology, was also the land where modern archaeology served its apprenticeship. There, within little more than a century, unearthing history changed from a collector's hobby into a serious and

An 18th-century collector of vases finds a hoard of Roman examples in a tomb.

systematic study. Finding antiquities was no longer the sole purpose: increasing knowledge of man and his story was now the main quest.

But, as we have already noticed, while the picture of Greece was still being revealed, interest in the past was steadily widening in other directions. The techniques of excavation, of drawing, and of recording that archaeologists first used there were already being applied elsewhere. Not only the lands of the eastern Mediterranean but also those of Middle America were beginning to yield up the hidden secrets of their long, eventful histories.

Sheer chance took a hand in the beginning of archaeology in the New World. John Lloyd Stephens, born in 1805 in Shrewsbury, New Jersey, became in course of time a busy lawyer with little time for his hobby—the study of antiquities. When he found himself suffering with throat trouble he welcomed his doctor's suggestion of a tour in the Mediterranean and Eastern Europe. The result was two travel books, works that quickly became classics of their kind.

Back home, in 1839, Stephens was delighted when the president sent him on a diplomatic mission to Middle America. He was already familiar with the works of Dupaix and de Waldeck, who a few years earlier had written accounts of this area; he also knew of an early 18th-century traveler's story of strange and very old buildings that were to be found in the depths of the Honduras jungle.

His chosen traveling companion was an Englishman, Frederick Catherwood, an accomplished artist with much experience of drawing

ancient buildings. They made an ideal pair. Willingly they journeyed all over Guatemala seeking the government to which Stephens was said to be accredited but which he could never find.

The nightmare journey was beset with difficulties. The countryside was in revolt and food was scarce. All around was the green wilderness of the jungle, impenetrable until a way had been cleared with an ax. Mules and baggage sank deep in muddy swamps; thorn bushes and mosquitoes made progress wearying.

Yet the two men persisted until at last, at Copan☞ in Honduras, they saw, covered by jungle growth, a long flight of stone steps. Hacking vines and tree roots as they went, they climbed the steps and came out onto a wall and a broad terrace hidden by centuries of tree growth. The explorers had found a temple of the ancient Mayas☞. They did not know when or by whom it was built; nor did the Indian who owned the building. Never having seen the ancient city that stood on his estate, he sold the whole site to Stephens for a mere 50 dollars.

On his return, Stephens published a book about his travels. Illustrated with Catherwood's fine and detailed drawings, carefully made on the spot, it was translated into several languages and excited keen interest, in both the New World and the Old.

Many people turned once more to the records of early Spanish settlers who had written with first-hand knowledge of the old civilizations of Central America; others took up the work of exploration and rediscovery that Stephens had begun.

Two of Catherwood's drawings depict Mayan monuments in all their elaborate detail. Left, a carved stone at Copan; below, ruins at Tuluum, Yucatan.

In the light of modern knowledge, the conclusions that Stephens drew are no longer accepted, but his keen observation made him the real founder of Mayan archaeology. Had it not been for the New York lawyer with his sore throat the knowledge we now have of Mayan civilization might not have been achieved for many years.

While Mayan archaeology was still in its early infancy, the story of a far older civilization was being unraveled in Western Asia.

Mesopotamia, the land between the rivers Euphrates and Tigris, was by tradition regarded as the site of the Garden of Eden. There, between the Mediterranean and the Persian Gulf, astride the chief trade route of the ancient world, great and famous empires once flourished. Of the cities of those empires nothing remained but mysterious flat-topped mounds in the desert.

There were no visible remains of temples and palaces to appeal to the imagination and set people working on a thorough search. But from the 16th century onward, occasional European travelers had brought home odd curios: tablets of clay inscribed in a strange wedge-shaped script.

A German college lecturer named Grotefend had begun to decipher the ancient scripts of Mesopotamia as early as 1802, but his work did not gain much recognition until years afterwards. The most spectacular part in the decipherment was played, some 40 years later, by the British orientalist Sir Henry Rawlinson.

Working precariously, far above ground level, he and his native helpers made careful copies of ancient inscriptions carved on a rock at Behistun, in Persia. These inscriptions carried the same message in three different languages—Old Persian, Elamite, and Babylonian. Starting from a few royal titles known in Old Persian, it was possible for Rawlinson to work back to an understanding of the older, but related, scripts. In this way a key was provided that, soon after serious excavation began, was to unlock a vast storehouse of knowledge about the cradle of civilization.

In 1842 a French physician, turned diplomat, became the pioneer of excavation in Mesopotamia—a work that was to continue for more than a century. Through the memorable explorations of Paul Botta, which were officially supported by the French government, the world first began to add to its meager knowledge of these ancient lands. It was Botta who, from the long-buried palace of an Assyrian king, unearthed the magnificent stone sculptures and relief carvings that now form a famous exhibition in the Louvre, in Paris.

Meanwhile, Austen Henry Layard, an Englishman whose early dreams of the East were influenced by the stories of the *Arabian Nights*, was making his own way to Mesopotamia, with the object of excavating the mound of Nimrud☞. With the help of a few Arabs he was at once successful. First Layard noticed a single large slab of stone; by the end

Layard's drawing, from an Assyrian relief, shows how giant statues were moved.

of a morning's work he had found a whole room. Success followed success, and in time the mound was found to cover the palaces of three Assyrian kings who had ruled at different periods between 883 and 669 B.C. As Layard's work progressed, several priceless treasures, now housed in the British Museum, were revealed—a black stone obelisk☞ recording in script and sculpture the main events of the reign of King Shalmaneser III (about 859-824 B.C.); giant winged bulls carved out of stone; enormous sculptures of human-headed lions.

During another expedition Layard discovered the palace of King Sennacherib with its great library of clay tablets. The work of the decipherers made it possible to read what proved to be prayers, incantations, stories, scientific texts, legal reports, and official letters, all of which shed new light on one small corner of human history.

The old civilizations of the Nile Valley were never forgotten as completely as those of Mesopotamia; throughout the ages they have proclaimed their grandeur through the Sphinx☞, the pyramids☞, and the ruins of mighty temples rising from the sands. Yet it was not until the end of the 18th century that everyday life in ancient Egypt began to be understood. Here, too, an inscription in three languages provided one of the main clues.

In his expedition to Egypt in 1798, Napoleon Bonaparte included among his army geographers, scientists, and skilled draughtsmen whose duty it was to collect and study antiquities. Nothing they found was to prove as important as the Rosetta Stone. This stone repeated a royal decree in hieroglyphic☞, in a script called *Demotic*☞, and in Greek. From the known Greek the two unknown scripts were deciphered, and in time many written records of Egypt were made plain.

By the middle of the 19th century much of the history of the Nile Valley was known. Thousands of papyri that had been meaningless now told of the arts and crafts, the customs and beliefs, the kings, priests, and prophets of ages long past. The chief monuments of ancient Egypt had always been familiar; but now the inscriptions they bore told of their purpose and of the men who built them. Nor was it only through writing that the past spoke to the present. Carvings, paintings, decorated tiles, and models from the tombs of kings all added to the message.

Often archaeologists concentrated on one small area of promise. Such an area was the site of El Amarna, some 200 miles south of Cairo. This once-great city was founded about 1375 B.C. by the Pharaoh Ikhnaton. It was occupied until only a short time after his death and was then abandoned. Slowly the shifting tide of sand overwhelmed it.

In 1898 Sir Flinders Petrie found at El Amarna the painted pavements of the harem of the Great Palace. In the years that followed, German and British archaeologists continued work on the site of the city. From the evidence they gathered it is now possible to picture some of the great buildings of El Amarna as Ikhnaton saw them more than 3000 years ago.

Egyptian tomb paintings show that fishing and fowling were favorite sports.

The excavations at El Amarna enable us to visualize one of the city's temples in Ikhnaton's day, and to picture life in the women's quarters of the palace.

Unearthing buried cities has not always been accomplished by archaeologists with a lifetime of study and training. In one very famous case it
was the achievement of a man who began his working life in a shop.

Heinrich Schliemann was born in 1822 at Schwerin in Mecklenburg,
north Germany, the son of a poor pastor who took a keen interest in
ancient history. When he was only seven years old, his father gave him
a book containing a striking picture of Aeneas—a legendary ancestor
of the Romans—fleeing from the horrors of burning Troy. From that
time on, Troy became an obsession with him. He found it almost im-
possible to believe that this once-powerful city had vanished, without
leaving so much as a clue to its whereabouts.

Most educated people of the day regarded the old Homeric stories of
Troy as no more than pleasing legends, for even Herodotus had found
no trace of the city, and learned men simply could not believe it had
ever really existed. Yet what others regarded as legend, Schliemann
accepted as fact. To find the lost city of Troy became the ruling passion
of his life.

It was an ambition not easily to be realized. There was no money in
the family to provide him with a classical education, and the dreamer of
Troy became first a grocer's apprentice and then a cabin-boy. After
suffering shipwreck off the Dutch coast he settled down as a book-
keeper to a firm in Amsterdam where, in an amazingly short time, he
mastered seven or eight foreign languages. His knowledge of Russian
led to an appointment in St. Petersburg (now Leningrad), and by 1847
Schliemann was already his own master. Thenceforth his career was
marked by one success after another. His various enterprises took him
to the United States, where he acquired American citizenship, then to
Egypt, Greece, Palestine, and Syria. Wherever he went he was quick to
seize business opportunities, and at the age of 41 he retired, a very
wealthy man.

In 1868, after a period of archaeological study in Paris and a spell of
world travel, Schliemann at last set out to search for Troy. The few
people who believed that the city really had existed thought it must
have stood near a village named Bunarbashi, in Asia Minor, but
Schliemann, relying on Homer, sought it nearer the coast. With the help
of a guide he came upon a flat-topped mound called Hisarlik that seemed
to him to fit Homer's description of the city's position.

There, for several seasons and with a hundred workmen to help him,
he went to work. At the end of his digging, when he struck bedrock, he
had laid bare the remains of nine successive decayed and buried cities,
one below another. None had previously been known, and Schliemann,
discoverer of Homeric Greece, became world-famous. On the very day
before work was due to cease, he and his Greek wife came upon priceless
gold treasures that had lain hidden since before the days of Troy.

An ancient vase painting shows Trojans defending their city against Greeks.

On catching sight of the first gleam of gold, nearly 30 feet below ground, Schliemann sent away all his helpers. Only he and his wife remained, frenziedly cutting ancient gold from beneath an ancient wall, heedless of the danger of falling masonry; and together they unearthed—and later succeeded in smuggling out of the country—a golden treasure of great historical value.

Although Schliemann was mistaken as to which of his nine cities was Homer's Troy, the grocer's boy had nevertheless added a thousand years to history.

The century in which Schliemann lived witnessed a revolution in ideas about man's place in a past far more distant than that of Troy.

It began with a renewed interest in old reports of stone tools that had been discovered near the remains of extinct animals, deep down in cave deposits. Knowing approximately how long nature takes to build up such deposits, geologists realized that these remains belonged to a very remote period indeed. Here was a new field of study: that of men who had lived before history began.

One of the leaders in the study of prehistory was Boucher de Perthes, a French customs officer who became interested in antiquities thrown up during the dredging of the Somme Canal. About 1837 he turned his attention to the local gravel pits, where he found many hundreds of flaked flint axes, and with them the bones of reindeer, bears, and the long-extinct mammoth.

By 1859, after a prolonged period of doubt, the learned world accepted his discoveries as authentic; de Perthes had proved that man existed far longer ago than had previously been believed.

Meanwhile, knowledge of early man had been greatly furthered by a Dane named Christian J. Thomsen who, in 1819, became curator of the Danish National Museum. Interested in antiquities since his early boyhood, Thomsen now shared his enthusiasm with visitors to the museum, and especially with country folk who, in their work on the land, might well unearth further evidence of early man. But his most important work was the classification of prehistoric implements according to the materials from which they were made. His theory that a Stone Age☞, a Bronze Age☞, and an Iron Age☞ mark three successive stages in man's development was to become a cornerstone of archaeology. The theory was proved sound by excavation☞, and thenceforth gave a rough-and-ready guide to the comparative age of prehistoric tools and weapons.

The man who perhaps helped more than anyone else to place the study of prehistory on a scientific basis was the British army officer, General Pitt-Rivers. Some people still look on him as the greatest of all archaeological excavators. An investigation into the history of the rifle, undertaken during his time in the army, led Pitt-Rivers to an interest in the evolution of tools, boats, dress, and all kinds of weapons. In 1880, when he inherited a fortune and a large estate in the west of England, he began a series of skilled excavations of prehistoric and Roman villages, forts, and burial grounds, and these became models for all future work of this kind.

Always he insisted on great care and precision: exact three-dimensional records must be kept, even to the point of boredom, to ensure that everything he found could be reconstructed on paper. For him a photograph of a skull was not sufficient for the records; he invented an instrument called a *craniometer*, with which he could measure such finds, with great exactness, at many different angles.

By such painstaking and methodical work he was able to throw much new light on primitive men, their appearance, their possessions, and the way they lived. He was also, perhaps, the first archaeologist to realize that, in recreating the past, the humble and ordinary things may count every bit as much as the grand and impressive ones.

During the 19th century, the man in the street was already getting to know about the work of archaeologists, but not until the 1920s did he share the thrill of a great discovery.

To Howard Carter, the discovery of the tomb of the youthful pharaoh Tutankhamen was the climax of six seasons of carefully planned, though unrewarded, work. To the public it was a sensational news item, proclaimed in bold headlines and broadcast from the newly

Photographs show the opening of the fourth shrine in Tutankhamen's tomb; the gold mask of the royal mummy; and the chest that contained the king's organs.

opened radio stations. Backed by Lord Carnarvon, an enlightened patron, and eagerly followed by representatives of the world's press, Carter popularized archaeology as had never been done before.

His success as an excavator owed much to sheer thoroughness—for instance to digging down to the solid rock, so as to uncover every possible feature of archaeological interest. In the side of a small hillock, he at last discovered 16 steps leading down to what he knew must be a tomb. Below was a heavily plastered door bearing the royal seals of the pharaoh Tutankhamen.

Within was an antechamber, filled to overflowing with a mass of decorated boxes, vases, statues, and royal furniture, and even the royal throne. This room was just as the tomb-robbers had left it many centuries before. Beyond were two other sealed chambers. The larger, opened with great ceremonial in 1923, housed the golden shrine of the king. Here, later, was seen the royal mummy☞, enclosed within three coffins. The inner one, of solid gold, needed eight men to lift it. As sheer bullion its value is enormous, but as a work of art it is beyond price, a great masterpiece of the goldsmith's craft.

An adjoining treasury contained incalculable wealth. As Carter gazed through the doorway, he saw, guarded by a statue of the god Anubis, the richly decorated shrine containing the king's organs, removed by the embalmers when the body was prepared for burial. Near by were the king's chariots, his hunting bow, his personal jewels, and even his sandals. Here, too, were statues of guardian gods; little effigies of servants of the dead to do the king's will in the afterworld; models of a granary and a mill, to supply his food; model ships in which he could follow the voyages of the sun across the heavens; chests containing his clothing; and caskets filled with weapons.

Why did Carter's discovery fire popular imagination the world over? Much was already known about other Egyptian kings far more powerful than Tutankhamen. Yet here, for the very first time, was revealed the full splendor of an Egyptian royal burial; now, at last, men of our own age could gaze on the face of a long-dead pharaoh.

Finds as spectacular as that of Tutankhamen's tomb are rare. More often the story of the past is built up from scattered fragments that, to the untrained eye, seem meaningless. From such scraps of evidence, discovered not only by excavators but also by other people who work close to the land, archaeologists have gleaned much knowledge about the early inhabitants of America.

The first Americans of all, we now think, migrated from Asia by way of the Bering Strait, perhaps as long ago as 20,000 years, when a land-bridge probably connected eastern Siberia and western Alaska. In both lands great deposits of bones of the same kinds of extinct animals have been found. In the frozen mud deposits of the Yukon Valley, in Alaska, gold-miners have also found, deep down in the soil, remains of extinct mammals associated with the flint points with which early hunters tipped their spears and arrows.

These primitive hunters were but the first arrivals. They were already men of modern type, for the earlier stages of man's development had taken place in the Old World. After them came others, some of whom, slowly and over centuries, made their way down the valleys and plains of North America, traveled through the narrow land-belt of Panama and eventually reached the southern continent. These men left their traces in many parts of the United States. In New Mexico, a cowboy found some flint tools and the bones of an extinct type of bison. Tusks, marked by primitive hunters, have been discovered in Florida. Deep plowing in Texas uncovered the bones of an American elephant, killed or wounded long ago by a stone spearhead.

In the New World, as in the Old, hunting was succeeded by farming, the foundation on which many widely differing civilizations were built. A great deal has been learned about the Mayas☞ of Yucatan, the Aztecs☞ of Mexico, the Incas☞ of Peru, and the Pueblo people of the southwestern United States, who lived in cliff dwellings and villages of stone; but there remain gaps in our knowledge of the origins of these peoples and how each came to build up its own highly individual way of life. Nor is there yet much that is certain about the Vikings of the old Icelandic sagas who, during the 10th century, made almost unbelievable journeys across northern waters from Iceland and Greenland to the northeast of America.

A 19th-century painting shows how Mandan Indians danced before a bison hunt.

It may well be that in North America discoveries as exciting as any yet made in the Old World still await the archaeologist. Meanwhile business concerns and private individuals, as well as professional and amateur archaeologists, are adding to our knowledge.

Not many years ago, workmen laying a new pipeline for a natural gas company discovered a large buried Pueblo village. Archaeologists, taken on the company's payroll, were able to make a proper excavation of the site.

Progress, too, is being made in dating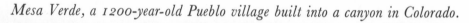 antiquities. One method, developed in America, is called tree-ring dating. The thickness of growth-rings in a tree depends on weather conditions during the growing season. The 10 rings of a 10-year-old tree vary in thickness just as the outer 10 rings of one 50 years old. In the same way, the inner 10 rings of the 50-year-old match the outer 10 of a still older tree. By matching up a chain of older and older trees it is possible to work out the age of timber used in ancient Indian buildings. Another new method of dating remains is by measuring how much radioactive carbon they have lost.

Throughout the world, archaeology is revealing ever more of man's buried past. In some areas it is concerned with prehistory; in others it is providing a background to historical events.

Mesa Verde, a 1200-year-old Pueblo village built into a canyon in Colorado.

In the Near East, excavation adds constantly to our knowledge of the everyday life that lay behind the Bible stories. For instance, diggers have laid bare Herod the Great's imposing hilltop palace at Masada. Wall paintings, pieces of masonry, carvings in ivory, and metal furnishings dating back to the days of King Solomon, deepen our understanding of temple architecture and decoration at the time of this most famous of all temple builders. At Byblos, north of Tyre, remains of temples more than a thousand years older than that of Solomon have been unearthed.

On the site of Jericho, the city that fell to the armies of Joshua, the remains of several ruined cities have been explored. One of the strangest of all the finds made there was that of human skulls, thought to be some 7000 years old, on which features were modeled in plaster, and shells inserted into the eye-sockets. Were these "sculptures" trophies of war or were they tributes to ancestors? The answer is not yet known.

Chance played a part in one of the least expected discoveries in this area of the world. For many years travelers have noticed strange carvings, often showing hunting scenes, on rocks in the Negev Desert, in southern Israel. Until recently they were taken to be the work of modern Bedouin Arabs. Then the members of a geographical expedition found that some of them were accompanied by inscriptions such as no

An aerial view of Masada, showing the remains of Herod the Great's palace.

modern Bedouin Arab would make. Archaeologists made further investigations and discovered that these inscriptions were in four different languages. The earliest of the inscribed carvings date back to 300 years before Christ; others, without inscriptions, may have been made much earlier.

The Treasure of Panagurishte, one of the most magnificent finds of recent years, was discovered by three brothers who were digging clay for bricks in southern Bulgaria. Nine vessels of solid gold were found buried seven feet deep in the ground. Some of the reliefs on these vessels, almost 2500 years old, depict gods and heroes of ancient times. One shows Theseus who, according to legend, slew the Minotaur, the fabulous Cretan monster with the body of a man and the head of a bull.

Little more than a century ago, the interior of Africa was unexplored. Yet there, more perhaps than anywhere else, archaeology is now probing the earliest mysteries of man's development.

On the borders of what are now Zambia and Tanzania, excavators recently examined the old beds of a lake that, because of changing rainfall through the ages, has altered its level several times. Buried at different levels were the tools of men who lived during the Early and Middle Stone Age. A careful comparison of finds from five different levels helped to show how early man's stone tools gradually improved.

Again in Tanzania, Dr. Louis Leakey and his wife Mary have unearthed man-like remains now known to be about 2,000,000 years old. On such evidence many experts feel sure that East Africa was where the ancestors of our own species had their beginnings.

In northeastern Europe, also, archaeologists are constantly finding examples of early man's crafts. From Finland, Lithuania, and northern Russia have come representations of human beings and more realistic carvings of animals in bone, wood, stone, and amber. Many of these date back to between 3000 and 4000 years ago when, in that area of the world, the Middle Stone Age was merging into the New Stone Age.

Today, however, archaeology goes much further than merely excavating and recording the traces of early man. Archaeologists have made films that vividly portray life in the Bronze Age. They have also reconstructed Iron Age houses and staged demonstrations there of how people lived and worked some 2000 years ago.

Tracking down the past is a process that goes on in all parts of the world. In the Altai Mountains of southern Siberia, archaeologists have discovered burial chambers long filled with ice. More than 2000 years ago, tribesmen used this burial ground for their leaders and great men. Throughout the years the ice has wonderfully preserved not only the fully clad bodies but also many of the treasures buried with them, including a carpet that may well be the oldest pile carpet in the world. Its design, in common with that of several richly figured wall hangings,

Part of a 2000-year-old wall hanging, from the graves of the Altai Mountains.

closely resembles those used in the Middle East, while the presence of silken goods indicates that these long-dead tribesmen of southern Siberia almost certainly had some contact with China.

Hundreds of tombs, some almost as old as those in the Altai Mountains, were discovered some years ago while a reservoir was being constructed in central China. Wall paintings and carvings found there give interesting glimpses of the life, costume, and crafts of the time.

It was in China, too, that a clue from an unlikely source led to one of the most important discoveries of the present century. For many years Chinese apothecaries have sold crushed "dragon bones" as a medicine. About 1900, German naturalists, studying quantities of these bones that they had bought in drug stores of the Far East, recognized them as the remains of extinct animals. Twenty years later, geologists began a search for their source. It was discovered that the bones came from a cave not far from Peking, and with them were found the fossil bones of many representatives of an extinct type of primitive man, together with weapons that he used for hunting and tools with which he dressed his meat. In fact this was the earliest kind of toolmaking man of whom we have a clear picture.

The "dragon bones" were the means of proving what was formerly unknown: that man must have lived in China in the exceedingly remote past.

4 Method and Science

What are the techniques by which archaeology rounds out and pushes further back in time the story of mankind? As in other sciences, methods are changing and improving all the time. But two essentials remain: critical observation and extreme care in recording.

These qualities are outstanding in the long career of a great Frenchman, the Abbé Henri Breuil. By the age of 20 he was already familiar with the flint tools of the Old Stone Age and with a number of the caves that prehistoric men had once used as homes or as temporary shelters. It was the spectacular rock paintings and engravings in these caves that claimed more and more of the Abbé's interest and that were later to become the subject of his life's work.

In 1901, with other investigators, he visited the now-famous caves of Font-de-Gaume and Combarelles, in southwestern France. Thanks to his tireless research, the superb paintings he saw there were for the first time recognized as examples of man's earliest pictorial art.

For many years the Abbé copied and traced primitive paintings and drawings, traveling widely in Europe, China, Ethiopia, and, later, in South Africa. His careful and sensitive records were often obtained under conditions of almost unbelievable hardship. He spent nearly 10 years in copying the engravings at Les Trois Frères.

It is mainly to the discovery and interpretation of the Abbé Breuil that we owe our knowledge of the first chapter of the history of art. Man's first pictures are chiefly concerned with animals—the mammoth, bison, ox, horse, and reindeer that were the familiar quarry of the Old Stone Age hunters. The few human beings who appear are usually engaged in hunting or in ritual dances, or else are disguised in animal masks. From these associations there is little doubt that the pictures had a magic purpose: most probably they were intended to ensure success in the chase, for the cave dwellers were dependent on hunting for their supplies of meat, hides, bones, and fur.

A prehistoric painting of a group of stags, found in the cave at Lascaux.

Many cave paintings display a combination of energy, animation, and realism that only the best of our modern film-cartoonists achieve. Some—especially the simpler rock drawings, like those shown here—also have the modern cartoonist's sparing use of line as well as his humorous touch.

When we realize how the cave artist painted, we are struck by the wonder, as well as the beauty, of his work. He had no palette, no prepared paints, and no brushes. For his tints he used graphite, red and yellow ocher, vegetable stains, and perhaps blood. The pigment was usually spread on as a fat-thickened paste, with crushed twigs, a moss pad, or the fingers, but sometimes it was blown onto the rock surface as a powder. And all the time the artists worked in darkness, lit only by the flickering flame of a crude stone lamp.

The classical areas of cave art are the mountains of southern France and northern Spain. The best-known cave, at Lascaux in the Dordogne, was found in 1940 by schoolboys. There the French archaeologist, F. Windels, has used the camera to make worthy records of some of the most magnificent paintings produced by early man.

No matter how careful the archaeologist may be in observing and recording, his work will yield the best results only if he has a lively sympathy with the past and instinctively feels it as a reality.

It is not enough, for example, for him to be able to recognize and classify 17 kinds of Saxon brooch: he must always be conscious that each

Grid excavation: undisturbed earth may later give clues to the wall's history.

was once pinned on a dress, that each could prick its owner's finger. Whatever advanced scientific techniques he may enlist in finding, preserving, or dating☞ antiquities, the archaeologist himself must provide that quality of thought and feeling that alone can span the time interval between earlier people and those of our own age.

This has been the firm belief of Sir Mortimer Wheeler, a leading British archaeologist whose search for the past lasted over half a century and took him all over the world—from Roman Caerleon and Verulamium in Britain, to the hill-forts of Normandy and Brittany, to the sites of ancient settlements in the Indus Valley and southern India, and to the Greco-Roman trading stations on the east coast of Africa.

Sir Mortimer thus summed up the point and purpose of his long and fruitful work: "We are not digging up things, but people."

Sixty years ago he found archaeology an almost unorganized study. The remarkable change that has taken place since then is due entirely to people like himself—to their mastery of technique, and to the importance they place on teaching it to others.

In the 1930s an Institute of Archaeology was founded in London, largely on Sir Mortimer Wheeler's initiative, for the training of students. About this time similar institutes were springing up in other old-established European nations and in America.

Here was another great step forward. Almost for the first time it was realized that the careful methods practiced by experienced archaeologists could be taught and applied to almost any kind of archaeological

Finds may be rusty, like this clasp; X-ray photography revealed its design.

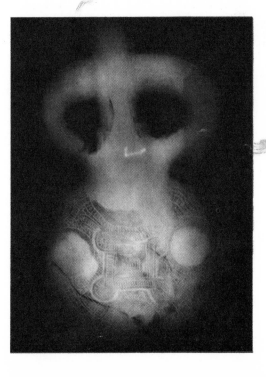

Soil layers show levels of occupation; paving gives a clue to a city's plan.

problem. They could be used not only in such places as Britain, which stood on the edge of the ancient world, but also in the areas where early civilizations reached their peak.

Teaching institutions have now been founded in many lands. Thus today, before the young archaeologist begins digging on an important site he is already well grounded in his profession. He understands the essentials of surveying, the various techniques of excavation☞, of sorting and classifying his finds; he knows just how and where photography can help him, when to call in a specialist in decipherment☞, what equipment to use in cleaning and preserving delicate ornaments before they are moved from a site.

He knows there is no one master method of excavation, and that he must consider the problems of each site as they arise. Where the site is known to have been inhabited, an area excavation based on a grid of squares is commonly used. Trial trenches are sometimes dug as a preliminary. Deep and wide trenches are used to test and reveal the sequence of structures, especially in fortifications.

But there is another side to teaching. Most of today's leading archaeologists have never forgotten that the story of bygone times is our common heritage. In words that we can all understand, in books, by radio, and by television, they bring the living past to our own firesides.

Perhaps Sir Mortimer Wheeler had this in mind when he said, "Sweating with the pen is no less important than sweating with the spade."

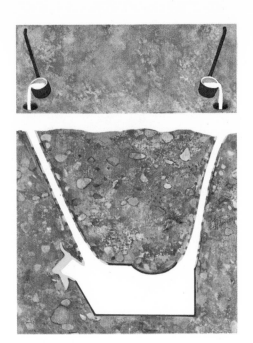

Plaster poured into holes at Ur formed the cast of a harp like those in mosaics.

Another great believer in the value of teaching and training was Sir Leonard Woolley, who between 1922 and 1934 directed the joint British and American expedition to Ur☞. He knew that the area likely to yield the most important finds was the Royal Cemetery. Even with an accomplished archaeologist constantly supervising, the task of excavating so promising a site could not well be left to any but the most highly skilled diggers. Woolley therefore postponed work on the Cemetery for two years, meanwhile concentrating on less vital areas where his assistants could more safely gain experience.

With a highly skilled team of workers and with very simple equipment, Woolley succeeded in preserving many valuable objects that, with a little less care, might easily have been destroyed. Antiquities that had suffered decay under the salt-laden soil of Ur were given "first-aid treatment" on the spot, so that technical specialists in museum laboratories could later ensure their preservation or reconstruct them.

The story of Queen Shub-ad's sledge-chariot shows what remarkable results this sort of first-aid treatment can give. The first sign of this beautiful piece of furniture was a golden mask, in the shape of a lion's head, standing upright in the earth. Close by it were the loose fragments of a strip of mosaic in shell and lapis lazuli. The fragments were covered with melted wax and no attempt was made to move them until the wax had hardened, holding them firmly in position; then the whole resulting strip was bound and reinforced with muslin. Further cautious digging uncovered more inlay work, which was treated in the same way, and more golden masks. At every stage of the work, notes of measurements were made and photographs taken, until it became clear that both masks and mosaic had once been fixed to a wooden framework that had long since rotted away. From the archaeologists' detailed records, a new framework was made; masks and mosaic were attached to it just as they had been to the original. In this way a complete reconstruction was built up.

On another occasion, in one corner of a royal tomb, excavators uncovered other fragments of mosaic work, loose in the soil and scattered at various levels. The mounting on which they had once been fixed had perished. Here again careful first aid was applied with wax and muslin. Patient and very detailed laboratory work followed. The result was the famous Standard of Ur, a banner of mosaic work made to be carried aloft on a pole, and decorated with priceless contemporary pictures of the Sumerian army.

Equally dramatic is the story that begins with the finding of two curiously shaped holes in the ground. By filling them with liquid plaster, the excavators obtained a cast of a harp from the impression left by its decayed wooden framework.

Yet quite often preservation on the spot was little more than a dull, routine job. Inscribed clay tablets, caked with mud and softened by their long burial in the earth, were baked hard before any attempt was made to clean them. The fragile remains of human skeletons were treated with wax so that they could be moved just as they were found.

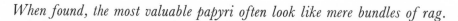

When found, the most valuable papyri often look like mere bundles of rag.

Such routine work, no less than the spectacular reconstructions, added their quota to our knowledge of the life, the written records, and the burial customs of a past civilization.

The rapid progress of archaeology during the present century is everywhere marked by fine teamwork; and very often people whose interests lie in quite different directions are called upon to become members of the team. That is what happened in 1939 when the most amazing archaeological discovery yet known in Britain was made at Sutton Hoo, near the coast of Suffolk.

In Saxon times a great, open, sea-going boat had been buried there in a trench dug in the sandy soil. In it were the magnificent treasures of a Saxon king: a bronze and iron helmet decorated in silver, a scepter, silver bowls and dishes, garnet-set gold jewelry, and a "standard" of iron bearing at its head a life-like bronze model of a stag. Boat and treasure were buried under a mound, long since covered with vegetation.

During the late 16th century, robbers had dug a shaft in an attempt to find the treasure, but happily they had missed it. Not until the 20th century was it to be revealed by the skill of modern archaeologists.

What kinds of people were involved in the work? First local archaeologists asked advice from the British Museum and from one of the large government departments—the Ministry of Works. Then professional archaeologists with special excavating experience took charge. A naval architect gave advice on the boat, a botanist on its timbers, and a soil

Great care is needed to separate the sheets and prepare them for decipherment.

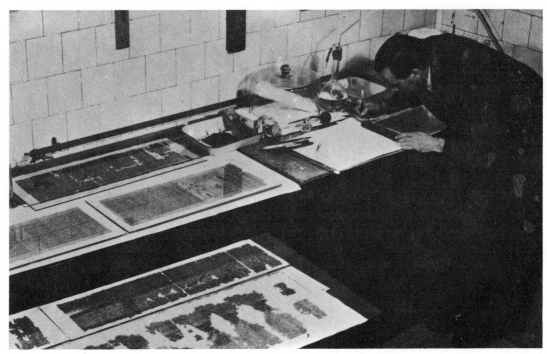

scientist on geological problems. The Ministry of Works lent special equipment. Expert photographers and draughtsmen recorded every stage of the excavation, during which police protection was given to the valuables. Cleaning, repair, and restoration of weapons, jewelry, woodwork, bone, leather, and textiles was undertaken by the scientists of the British Museum laboratory.

The team not only unearthed a treasure worth more than a quarter of a million pounds sterling, but also revealed a valuable page of Saxon history. The strange memorial they uncovered was not a grave but a cenotaph, for no body was buried there. Yet 40 gold coins give a clue to the king in whose memory it was made. They date the burial of the ship to a period between A.D. 650 and 670, during which two notable East Anglian kings died: Anna, in 654, and Aethelhere, killed in battle, in 655.

Several of the dead king's valued possessions were heirlooms handed down from the days of the Norse sagas, which had seen the origin of the royal house. Two silver spoons bearing, in Greek, the names Saul and Paul—reminders of St. Paul's conversion—were probably a present to mark the king's own conversion to Christianity.

A large collection of silver bowls, dishes, and ladles of various dates, from Eastern Europe and the Middle East, indicate something of the trade connections of Saxon England. Among other finds were drinking horns and caldrons, reminders of the feasting scenes in the Anglo-Saxon epic poem *Beowulf*.

Excavators at Sutton Hoo revealed the outline of a Saxon ship; its contents included a king's helmet, his drinking horn, and the lid of his purse (above).

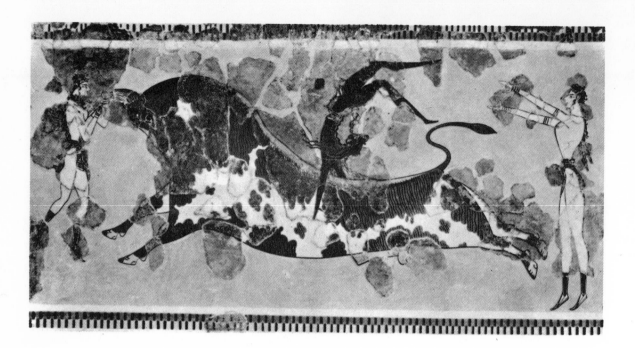

A wall painting in Minos's palace shows a man somersaulting over a bull's back.

But the greatest triumph at Sutton Hoo was the investigation of the ship itself. The timbers had rotted away, leaving nothing but iron nails and stains in the sand. Patiently the unstained sand around them was carved and brushed away until the very ghost of a ship remained: ribs, strakes, gunwales were all outlined in the natural soil.

From this evidence the lines of a ship of the period were reconstructed. Teamwork had given substance to a ghost and brought a piece of dead history to life.

Some of the most fascinating and tantalizing problems of archaeology are those concerned with early forms of writing: fascinating because ancient documents may suddenly floodlight a dark corner of the past; tantalizing because they may defy all attempts at decipherment for many years, as happened in the case of the inscribed clay tablets of ancient Crete☞.

Until the end of last century, little was known about the civilizations that flourished in Crete between 3000 and 5000 years ago. Then, in 1900, Sir Arthur Evans began his excavations on the site of the city of Knossos☞, during which he unearthed the vast and complex palace of the Cretan sea-kings, the famous Palace of Minos. At the peak of its grandeur, about 1500 B.C., the palace had contained throne room, council chamber, workshops, huge warehouses for the storage of wine and oil, and luxurious living quarters fitted with elaborate water-supply and drainage systems. Beautiful wall paintings, fine statues and carvings,

An example of Linear A, a Minoan script that still defies all attempts at interpretation.

even the decoration on gigantic storage jars, all spoke of a high state of civilization. Yet many hundreds of inscribed clay tablets added nothing to our knowledge of ancient Crete until years after their discovery, because it was not possible to decipher them.

At various periods the ancient Cretans used three different scripts. The last-developed of these, in use just before the destruction of Knossos, and called "Linear B," long defied all attempts at interpretation. In deciphering the scripts of Egypt, scholars had had the help of the Rosetta Stone. Here there was no such clue. How, then, was the problem to be tackled?

The answer was finally found by a young English architect, Michael Ventris. For years he worked patiently, both alone and with others, using many of the highly technical systems of the trained cryptographers, or code breakers. The fact that "Linear B" consisted of about 70 common signs made him think that each stood for a different syllable, since several languages make use of about 70 syllables. The fact that similar inscriptions had been found on the Greek mainland suggested that the language of Crete might have some connection with that of ancient Greece. Ventris examined hundreds of inscriptions, analyzing how frequently the various signs occurred, noting how often they formed certain recognizable groups, watching for any clue that might hint at sound-values or meanings. In time he drew up a table giving to each sign a sound-value that occurred in ancient Greek. If his table were correct the inscriptions should now make sense.

He put theory to the test. Part of one inscription, thus translated, read: "Horse-vehicle, painted red, with bodywork fitted, supplied with reins." This certainly made sense and so did many others. Ventris's feat of decipherment has been called "the Everest of Greek archaeology."

So far the inscriptions found have proved to be little more than lists of goods. But if the day comes when more of Crete's written history is unearthed, it will at once be plain to read.

Today the past yields up its secrets not only to the excavator digging down into the earth but also to the cameraman flying high above it. In southern Europe and in Tunis, air photography☞ has added much to our understanding of prehistoric settlements, Etruscan tombs, and Roman farms. In Scotland, a new air reconnaissance has increased our knowledge of that frontier area of the Roman Empire to such an extent that part of its history has had to be written afresh.

How is it that the camera gives such a clear picture from the air of what is hardly noticeable from the ground? One answer lies in a peculiar property of the ground itself. Once soil has been disturbed it seldom settles precisely as compactly as the undisturbed soil around it.

Imagine a prehistoric food-storage pit. It serves its purpose, falls into disuse, and collapses. By a natural process of silting, it gradually fills up until there is nothing to mark where it was. Many centuries pass by and the site becomes a field, yielding crops year after year. One spring it is sown with wheat. The soil in the disused pit, lighter in texture than that

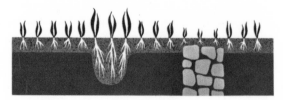

Seen from the air, crop marks reveal site of a neolithic village. Crops grow higher above filled-in ditches; their growth is stunted above ruined walls.

around it, holds moisture and encourages a fine growth of young wheat. From ground level the difference in the quality of the crop may be scarcely visible, but from the air, the patch of more luxuriant growth is conspicuous, often with a characteristic shape of its own.

Shallow soil, on the other hand, hinders growth by cramping roots and dispersing moisture. Buried structures such as roads and walls permit above them only areas of stunted growth which, especially during a drought, show on an air photograph as lines and streaks.

Wheat, oats, barley, and rye are helpful crops to the archaeologist; roots, woodland, and scrub are useless. The nature of the subsoil, too, is important. Differences in growth show up well in chalk or limestone, poorly in sand, clay, or loose gravel. Season and quality of light must also be considered. It is useless to look for crop marks after harvest, when only the stubble remains; spring, when growth has just begun, and summer when crops are ripe, are far better.

When the sun is low, irregularities in the ground-surface, even slight ones, cast quite long shadows. Air photographs taken at such a time often reveal features hardly visible to a ground observer. Burial mounds, roadways, and lost villages may then be recognized for the first time. What the camera reveals in outline, the excavator can later examine in detail.

Where part of a site has already been dug, an air photograph may reveal a clear ground plan and thus show where further digging would be likely to give the best results.

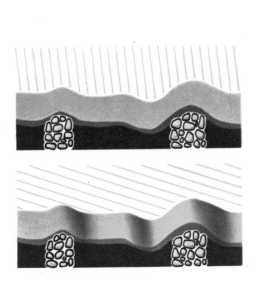 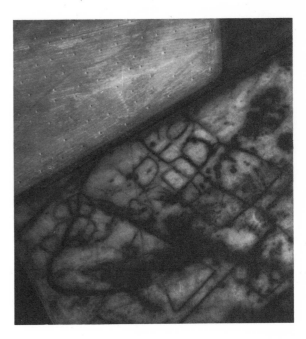

Crop marks show site of an iron-age settlement. Long shadows cast by sun's rays near dawn and sunset (diagram) may reveal earthworks invisible at noon.

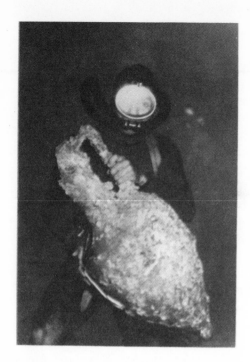

When divers locate sunken wine jars, or a submerged building, they square the site off with cord. Then they photograph the finds and record their positions.

In studying the past, the archaeologist takes full advantage of every useful device the present can offer. When the Frenchman Jean-Jacques Cousteau developed the aqualung—which made it possible for men to move unencumbered beneath the sea, and to remain under water for comparatively long periods—archaeologists quickly seized on it as a means of plucking history from the seabed.

Throughout the ages, storms have taken toll of men's ships; at times, too, the sea has flooded whole towns. Occasionally the sea gave back some small relic to the hands of a sponge diver or the net of a trawler. More rarely, tethered divers, taking their supply of air from above water, have fully explored a wreck, as in 1907 when French divers found a Greek galley, laden with works of art, that had sunk near Tunis 2000 years before.

Now, free diving opens up an exciting new field of archaeology. Along the south coast of France, off the shores of Italy, Spain, and North Africa, divers equipped with masks, flippers, and compressed air cylinders, constantly descend to the seabed to explore the remains of ships lost long ago. Pressurized cameras with flashbulbs make graphic on-the-spot records; television cameras transmit up-to-the-minute news to the surface. One American team of underwater archaeologists uses a 16-foot submarine, a one-man underwater capsule towed by a surface ship, and sonar apparatus to detect objects on the seabed.

Already much has been learned of the wine trade of ancient Greece and Rome. Thousands of wine jars, some with the inscribed wax seal of the shipper still in place, have been found. Occasionally the very timbers of the ship are recovered.

When a reconnaissance team discovers a submerged town, a large under-sea "dig" begins. Plastic cord is used to mark off the site into squares, so that detailed records can be made of the position of each find. In the case of a ship buried in ooze, a large, flexible suction-pipe clears away the overlying mud ready for the search to begin. Antiquities are often hauled to the surface in wire baskets.

This new technique is now practiced beyond the confines of the Mediterranean, chief shipping route of the ancient world. In Lake Titicaca, between Bolivia and Peru, an American free-diver discovered the ruins of Chiopata, an ancient city of the Incas. And in Middle America, divers using the latest scientific aids wrested remarkable objects from the depths of a Mayan sacrificial well.

One of the first questions that everyone asks the archaeologist is: "How old is it?" Atomic science has provided the most accurate answers.

Working at Chicago University, in the laboratories of the Institute of Nuclear Studies, Professor Willard F. Libby studied the formation of radioactive carbon in organic substances. He found that all plants, as they absorb carbon dioxide from the air, take in with it minute quantities of a radioactive form of carbon known to scientists as Carbon-14. Since all animals depend directly or indirectly on plants for their food, it follows that every living thing contains Carbon-14. But when an organism, whether animal or vegetable, dies, it normally takes in no further carbon. Instead, its radioactive carbon begins to decay.

In dead organisms the proportion of Carbon-14 decreases at a fixed rate that does not vary under any known physical conditions. After 5730 years, half the Carbon-14 content is lost; in the next 5730 years half the remainder disappears, and so on. By comparing the amount left in any dead organic matter with the amount in living matter, scientists can estimate when the organism died.

The process, which is complicated and requires highly specialized apparatus, is now long past its early experimental stage, but improvements are still being made. Briefly, suitable samples are first burned to form carbon dioxide gas. In one method, the gas, after further chemical treatment, is then treated with magnesium to produce pure carbon. Finally the carbon, in the form of a paste, is fed to a Geiger counter☞. The older the sample is, the less Carbon-14 it contains and the slower is the pulse of the Geiger counter.

What sort of things have already been examined in this way, and what has this very modern technique taught us?

The shell of a land-snail from Jarmo, one of the oldest villages in western Asia, is found to be over 6500 years old. Charcoal discovered in the entrance of the famous Lascaux cave in France proves to be the remains of a fire that burned some 15,000 years ago. Trees killed by the last ice age in North America died about 11,500 years ago. Before carbon dating began, geologists had thought that the last American ice age was much earlier.

Like every other archaeological method, radiocarbon dating still has limitations. Some kinds of organic material—and unfortunately bone is one of them—do not give such good results as others. Further, when organic material is much over 25,000 years old, its Carbon-14 content is too small to be measured accurately. Yet despite limitations this wonderful scientific aid is rapidly filling in many of the gaps that still exist in the story of the remote past.

It is not only nuclear physics that helps the archaeologist. Biology, botany, geology, and chemistry are also revolutionizing our approach to the past.

It was the geologist, with his specialized knowledge of various rocks and when they were formed, who first found a yardstick by which to measure past time. At first his scale, which measured time in millions of years, gave little help in dating the buried evidence of man: most human records belong to only the last few hundred thousand years. But now the last part of the geologist's scale has been divided into very much smaller units. In Sweden, geologists have found that as glaciers

The Qumran scroll was too brittle to unroll; experts cut it up with a saw.

partially melt each summer they leave behind a fine layer of sand or clay. These layers vary in thickness each year and, like the growth rings in trees, provide a method of dating.

By identifying almost indestructible grains of fossil pollen, the botanist can tell what crops early man grew and even in what climatic conditions he grew them. The zoologist knows when various animals of past times lived and when they became extinct. He can thus give a clue to the age of primitive weapons that are sometimes embedded in their remains.

Technical advances in many fields are enlisted in the work of archaeology. During the late 1940s a number of ancient written scrolls were discovered near the Dead Sea. One, made of copper, had become extremely fragile because of the chemical changes it had undergone over many years. Any attempt at unrolling might well have destroyed it. Expert mechanical engineers mounted the scroll on a spindle to avoid constant handling, coated the outside with strong adhesive to prevent crumbling, and used a special saw to cut it into slices. None of the uncorroded lettering was damaged.

Archaeologists have long used papier-mâché to take "squeezes" or impressions of inscriptions on old monuments. Now they can use liquid latex-rubber which, when it sets, gives a clearer impression, lasts longer, and is easier to move about.

Science provides the essential means of restoring and evaluating the genuine relics of early man; it also helps to prevent the archaeologist being taken in by false evidence.

"Piltdown Man" was reconstructed from bones (black and white) that had been buried as a hoax. The jaw was almost identical with an ape's (foot of page).

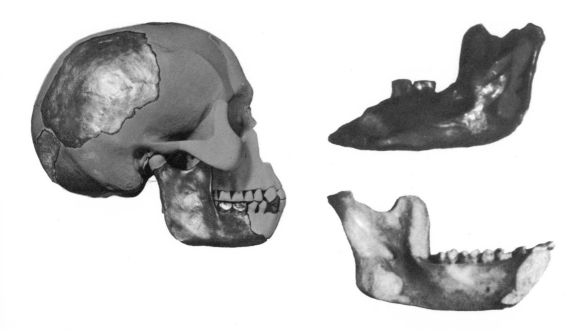

The greatest forgery ever made in archaeology, the production in 1912 of the remains of Piltdown Man, once claimed to be 500,000 years old, was detected 40 years later by the combined efforts of a whole team of scientists. Chemical tests proved that the skull contained much less fluorine than bones of that great age would normally contain. The presence of a chromium compound, used to give the bones the appearance of great age, was detected by X-ray spectrographic analysis. A close examination by expert anatomists suggested that the lower jaw was that of an ape.

With all the aids of modern science at its disposal, what has archaeology achieved? Nowhere, perhaps, can we see the answer more clearly than in the great national museums. There the once-scattered pieces of bygone times are gathered together and arranged with such skill that the past comes to life before our eyes.

To make this possible, a great deal of work has gone on behind the scenes. Museum authorities organize archaeological expeditions to all parts of the world. In laboratories and workshops, finds that have received first-aid treatment in the field undergo further cleaning and repairing. From fragments that the excavator has unearthed and from the records and measurements he has made, skilled craftsmen prepare accurate reconstructions and models of antiquities that have suffered damage or decay. Every object is dated as closely as possible and subjected to the most rigid tests to prove its authenticity.

Skill in arrangement matches skill behind the scenes. No longer are Roman and Egyptian vases casually put with stuffed animals, as they were in so many ill-lit museums of last century. Finds are grouped according to period, place, or culture, so that the group as a whole gives a clear picture of one aspect of man's history. Trained staff are always at hand to answer questions; specialists give every possible help in identifying antiquities brought in by visitors. There are conducted tours, lectures, demonstrations, and film-shows.

Yet no museum, however big, can fully cover the archaeology of all times and all places, and some therefore specialize in the past of one or two areas. Smaller museums may even concentrate on the detailed archaeology of their own districts. But for students whose interests go beyond the displays, there are usually rooms set apart for quiet study and libraries containing a wide range of reference books. There are also university museums in which teaching is the main purpose.

Thus museums not only preserve and show to everyone the heritage of the past; they also help in the training of those who will some day set out to solve the mysteries that remain. For, in spite of all that has already been achieved, there is no doubt that many exciting discoveries still await the archaeologist of the future.

In a museum gallery, purified air preserves the Parthenon sculptures from decay.

No one has yet read the inscription on the Cretan Disk of Phaestos or learned the meaning of some of the strange glyphs of Middle America. Archaeologists are still puzzled about the origin of certain prehistoric rock paintings found in Africa.

Secrets of the past are still hidden in the soil and in the sea. Many questions about early man remain unanswered. How did the first farmers arise—men whose reliable food supply made civilization possible? Why did the Eskimos stay in Arctic lands while other early Americans migrated southward? How did the aborigines of Australia, the Ainus of Japan, the Maoris of New Zealand, develop their special cultures?

The history of the last 10,000 years is fast unfolding, but further back man's story is still largely lost in the mists of time.

Glossary

In this Glossary, as in the rest of the book, the symbol ☞ means that the term it follows has its own alphabetical entry in the Glossary, to which you may refer for a fuller definition or for more information.

ABBEVILLIAN A Paleolithic☞ food-gathering culture that flourished roughly between 500,000 and 450,000 years ago. Its characteristic crude stone handaxes occur from southern Africa north to Britain, and northeast to Asia.

ABU SIMBEL The Sudanese site of monolithic Egyptian temples hewn from solid sandstone, notably the Great Temple of Rameses II (13th century B.C.).

A rescue operation to save the temple from flooding (caused by damming the Nile for irrigation purposes) has meant cutting it into blocks and rebuilding it on high ground.

ACHEULIAN A Paleolithic☞ food-gathering culture characterized by skillfully shaped stone handaxes, and some use of fire. It began in Africa about 400,000 years ago as a development of the Abbevillian☞ culture, and lasted over 200,000 years.

ACROPOLIS A hill-fort of any period or place, from a Greek word meaning "high city." The best known are those of Mycenae and Athens—both originating in Achaean times as defensive centers ruled by kings.

AIR PHOTOGRAPHY A technique for discovering and demonstrating archaeological sites. It depends largely upon the effects of ancient soil disturbance on vegetation patterns. Disturbed areas show up as shadows, highlights, parchmarks, or damp marks.

AMPHITHEATER A giant circle of tiered seats built on arched supports and enclosing a central arena. It was a Roman development of the Greek theater—a semicircle of tiered stone seats set into the natural curve of a hill. Rome's great amphitheatre, the Colosseum, held 45,000.

AMPHORA A two-handled pottery vessel used by the ancient Greeks and Romans for storing oil and wine.

ANGKOR WAT Part temple, part royal tomb, and reputedly the world's biggest religious building. It was raised in the 12th century A.D. by the Khmers of Cambodia—mongoloid southeast

Statue of Rameses II at Abu Simbel

Greek amphora

Assyrian battle techniques

An Assyrian king at war

Asians influenced by Indian forms of religion and architecture. They abandoned it by the 15th century after invasion by mongoloid Thais from the north. It remained neglected for four centuries.

ANTONINE WALL A 37-mile-long wall built across Scotland from the Firth of Forth to the Firth of Clyde by the Roman Emperor Antoninus Pius (A.D. 138-161) to relieve barbarian pressure on the wall built farther south by Hadrian☞. It was 14 feet wide, 10 feet high, and had 19 forts manned by Roman legionaries.

ARCHAEOMAGNETIC DATING A method of dating ancient kilns, hearths, and other baked-clay objects. Clay contains iron oxides in tiny particles that act as magnets, pointing in directions determined by the earth's magnetic field. Baked clay locks inside it a permanent record of the earth's magnetic field at the time of baking. But the earth's magnetic field varies over the centuries. So, by comparing the magnetic patterns in "new" and "old" clay, experts can say, for instance, just how old a Roman furnace may be.

ARTEFACT Any object made by the hand of man.

ASSYRIANS Semitic peoples named for the city of Ashur in what is now north Iraq. Between 2000-1000 B.C. they built a kingdom by force, using iron weapons and ruthless battle tactics. By the seventh century B.C. the Assyrian Empire stretched from the Mediterranean to the Persian Gulf. But combined attacks by Medes☞ and Chaldeans destroyed it in 612 B.C.

AURIGNACIAN An Upper Paleolithic☞ culture that flourished in western Europe in the first warm oscillation of the second advance of the Würm Ice Age☞. It featured fine stone blades, pins and awls of bone, fire, the first cave art, rudimentary religion, and evidently, speech. See MAGDALENIAN and SOLUTREAN.

AVEBURY The Wiltshire site of Britain's largest monolithic prehistoric monument, built by the Beaker People☞ about 1700-1500 B.C. It comprises more than 28 acres of earthworks and stone circles.

AZTECS American Indians of Middle America who established an empire straddling south and central Mexico about the 13th century A.D. Centered on the city of Tenochtitlan, it featured a powerful government, ritual mass-sacrifices, efficient agriculture, and splendid art. The Aztecs lacked a distinctive culture, adopting Toltec☞ religion, Mixtec☞ art, and a calendar from an unknown source. They were crushed in the early 1520s by a small Spanish force led by Hernando Cortes.

Aztec calendar stone

BABYLON Ancient Mesopotamian capital of Babylonia, developed about 2050-1750 B.C. by the Semitic Amorites, redeveloped in the fifth century B.C.—after destructive invasions—by the Semitic Chaldeans.

BARROW A mound of soil or rock covering a burial—common in pre-Roman Britain. "Barrow" stems from an Old English word that means "hill."

BEAKER PEOPLE The first Bronze-Age immigrants to Britain (about 1800 B.C.), named for their characteristic beaker-shaped pottery mugs. They modified Stonehenge☞ and built Avebury☞.

Vessel of the Beaker People

BRONZE AGE The period in cultural evolution between the Neolithic☞ and the Iron Age☞. People began working bronze (a tin-copper alloy less brittle than stone and harder than pure copper) in west Asia about 3000 B.C. Its use spread by diffusion but was eventually supplanted by that of iron.

BURIAL MOUND A mound or barrow☞ raised over a grave. Neolithic☞ long mounds and Bronze-Age☞ round mounds are well-known European examples.

CARTHAGE Phoenician city, center of a west Mediterranean trading empire, founded in 814 B.C. in northwest Africa and destroyed by the Romans in 146 B.C.

CHICHÉN ITZA One of the largest Mayan cities in the peninsula of Yucatan, founded about A.D. 250, taken by the Toltecs☞ about A.D. 1000,

Bronze-smelting in ancient Egypt

70

Treasures of Mycenae *Mycenae, named by Homer as Agamemnon's capital, was first excavated by Heinrich Schliemann in 1876. In graves, he found treasures like this sword blade and gold mask; made 400 years before Agamemnon, they revealed Mycenae as the center of a great prehistoric civilization.*

and deserted about A.D. 1200—possibly as a result of war. It is remarkable for an astronomical observatory, massive temples, a sacrificial well, and superb sculptures, mosaics, and murals.

Ancient Alexandrian coin

CHOUKOUTIEN AND SOAN Chopper tool cultures of east Asia. A lump of stone was broken by striking it with another stone. Both the residual core and the flakes struck from it were apparently used. This culture was perhaps developed by Pithecanthropus (see EARLY MAN) who evidently used fire. It may have given rise to the Clactonian☞ culture. See also OLDOWAN.

CLACTONIAN The first Paleolithic☞ culture, featuring fully developed flake tools☞ as opposed to core tools☞. It is named for finds at Clacton in Essex, England, but probably originated in Asia from the so-called Choukoutien☞ culture. It flourished from about 450,000 to 250,000 years ago and was produced by men of a now extinct species or group of species.

Clactonian hand ax

COINS Pieces of metal bearing an official stamp and used as money. The oldest certainly dated coins are electrum staters made in Lydia (now in Turkey) under King Gyges (about 685-652 B.C.). Coins abolished the time-wasting practice of weighing out precious metals for each transaction. Numismatology—the study of coins—helps to reveal facts about the affluence and trading links of extinct cultures.

COPAN A great Mayan city in Honduras, discovered by the 19th-century American archaeologist John L. Stephens.

CORE TOOLS Paleolithic☞ and Mesolithic☞ tools made of lumps of stone from which flakes have been struck. The best known core tools are the almond-shaped Acheulian☞ handaxes of flint and quartzite. See FLAKE TOOLS and FLINT.

CRETE A narrow, mountainous island 60 miles southeast of mainland Greece; the birthplace of European civilization.

Between 3000-2000 B.C. Cretans established eight cities that were based on east Mediterranean trade and politically unified, about 2000 B.C., by a so-called Minoan ruler.

Theseus slaying the Cretan Minotaur

How the cuneiform script was written

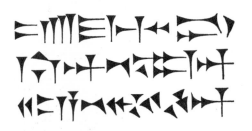

Copy of a cuneiform inscription

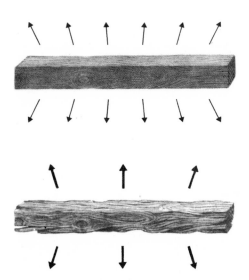

Radiocarbon tests enable scientists to date timbers: the radioactivity of timber diminishes with age.

About 1400 B.C. war or earthquake shattered the royal palaces, including Knossos☞, and Cretan civilization went into a slow decline.

CULTURE The customs, equipment, techniques, manufactures, ideas, and beliefs of a people or set of peoples. In short, all the patterns of behavior learned in a society.

CUNEIFORM Literally "wedge-shaped" writing, characteristic of the Sumerian☞ and succeeding west Asian civilizations.

By pressing the tip of a stylus into a soft clay tablet, a scribe made wedge-shaped marks that formed the basis of characters.

CURSUS A class of European Neolithic☞ monument consisting of long parallel banks flanked by ditches—running for miles in some cases and with squared or curved ends. Their function is not known.

DANUBIAN CULTURE The first Neolithic☞ European culture, named for the lower Danube area where it was emerging in 5000-4000 B.C.

It involved shifting agriculture and stock-raising and in time influenced virtually all of western Europe.

DATING Determining the age of an object.

Methods of dating animal remains include measuring their loss of radioactive carbon (i.e. Carbon-14 dating—valid for remains up to 70,000 years old) or potassium (i.e. potassium-argon dating, for remains millions of years old); assessing their accumulation of fluorine and uranium; and studying the magnetic pattern in their bone cells (it tallies with the earth's magnetic field at the time of each organism's death).

Methods of dating plant remains include Carbon-14, tree-ring correlations, and pollen analysis☞.

Methods of dating inorganic objects include the archaeomagnetic dating☞ of baked clays, counting varves (annual silt layers deposited by retreating glaciers), and assessing the loss of radioactivity of certain elements in rocks.

DATUM An arbitrarily fixed point from which all others are measured on an archaeological site.

The Buried City   *Pompeii, a flourishing Roman city, was suddenly buried under 45 feet of volcanic ash in* A.D. *79 . The ash preserved buildings—like the bakery above—and even the bodies of its victims.*

Early man

Easter Island statue

DECIPHERMENT Learning the meaning of inscriptions that are damaged or written in code or in an unknown script.

Decipherment can involve using special photographic equipment to reveal inscriptions damaged by corrosion; code-breaking systems devised by cryptographers; or correlation of an unknown script with a wide range of known scripts.

It was largely by reasoning from facts about known scripts that in 1952 the British architect Michael Ventris deciphered the puzzling Cretan script Linear B. More recently Soviet mathematicians employed computers to decipher a script of the Mayas☞.

DEMOTIC "People's" writing—a much-simplified Egyptian script (derived from hieratic and hieroglyphic☞) written from right to left, and in common use by the seventh century B.C. The French scholar Jean-François Champollion deciphered it in 1822 after comparing demotic, hieroglyphic, and Greek inscriptions on the Rosetta Stone.

EARLY MAN A word describing any Paleolithic☞ men, particularly the first toolmaking hominids —notably the Australopithecines of southern Africa and Pithecanthropus in east Asia.

EARLY STONE AGE See PALEOLITHIC.

EASTER ISLAND A small, remote island in the eastern Pacific Ocean, discovered by the Dutch explorer Jacob Roggeveen in 1722, but previously settled by Polynesians—probably originating in southeast Asia. Using stone tools and a rudimentary grasp of mechanics they erected remarkable monolithic stone statues.

ECBATANA An ancient city in what is now Iran. Founded by the Medes☞ about 700 B.C. as their capital, it became a major town within the Achaemenid Persian Empire. See PERSIA.

EOLITH From the Greek for "dawn stone"— describing kinds of pebble apparently crudely but deliberately shaped and once supposed to be the first man-made stone tools.

Modern research has shown that eoliths were probably formed entirely by natural means.

ETRUSCANS Bronze-using Caucasoid peoples who colonized northwest Italy about 900 B.C.—possibly as refugees from the disintegrating Hittite☞ Empire of Asia Minor.

They built fortified cities ruled by princes, wrote in a still largely undeciphered script, and painted remarkable tomb murals.

They were absorbed by Rome—politically by 300 B.C., culturally by the first century A.D.

EXCAVATION The methodical removal of debris covering archaeologically significant relics, by digging down to a predetermined depth in a carefully surveyed site—often using trowels and brushes to facilitate the detailed examination of the excavated material.

FERTILE CRESCENT A term coined in 1916 by the American archaeologist James Henry Breasted for a fertile belt from the southeast Mediterranean to the north of the Persian Gulf, bounded by mountains to the north and desert to the south. It supported some of the first farming settlements and the civilizations that they made possible.

FLAKE TOOLS Tools made from the flakes struck from a stone core. Flake arrowheads, knife blades, saws, and scrapers formed a vital part of toolkits in the Upper Paleolithic☞ and Mesolithic stages of man's cultural development. See also CORE TOOLS.

FLINT A hard, glassy rock of cryptocrystalline silica. Because flint readily shatters into hard, sharp-edged pieces, men used it extensively for making core☞ and flake tools☞.

FOSSILS Evidence in rock of the remains of dead plants and animals. The evidence may be their actual physical remains, the imprint of their bodies in rock (produced when the rock was in a soft state), or mineral deposits that by replacing their tissues have literally turned them to stone.

GEIGER COUNTER Named for the German physicist Hans Geiger (1882-1945)—an instrument for detecting and measuring particles or waves given off by a radioactive substance and used archaeologically in radioactive dating.

Etruscan warrior

Probing a cave with a Geiger counter

The Roman Emperor Hadrian

Egyptian hieroglyphics

GEOCHRONOLOGY A method of dating that combines the knowledge of geology, botany, zoology, and physics.

GLYPH A sculptured mark or symbol as on a Mayan stele☞. As a vertical groove in Doric friezes it figured largely in Greek architecture.

GRAVES, PASSAGE AND GALLERY The two main types of megalithic☞ tomb. A passage grave is a circular mound covering a narrow passage leading to a burial chamber. A gallery grave has no passage, and a long burial chamber.

GREEKS, ANCIENT Caucasoid, Indo-European-speaking peoples who entered Greece about 4000 years ago as warlike, bronze-using farmers, speaking an archaic form of Greek.

By 1600 B.C. so-called Achaean Greece held many small states—notably Mycenae. But only after contact with the old-established civilizations of Crete☞ and Egypt did the Greeks build their own classical civilization.

HADRIAN Roman Emperor (A.D. 117-138) who strengthened the Empire's defenses by walls built between the Rhine and Danube and across the north of England.

HARAPPA One of the two major cities established by the Indus Valley civilization☞ in what is now West Pakistan.

HENGES Monuments in Western Europe that date from the Neolithic☞ and Bronze Ages☞ periods. A henge consists of a round bank and ditch (or several of each) broken by one or more entrances. Some hold circles of standing stones☞ or have an avenue of stones leading in from outside. The two best-known henges are Avebury☞ and Stonehenge☞.

HIEROGLYPHIC Greek for "sacred carving" and applied to inscriptions by peoples of many civilizations but in particular to a script used on ancient Egyptian monuments and deciphered in 1822 by Champollion (see also DEMOTIC).

Early hieroglyphic symbols were all pictographic but modifications came to include hieroglyphs with phonetic values.

HILL-FORTS Iron-Age☞ hilltop settlements surrounded by protective earth walls and ditches.

HITTITE CIVILIZATION It flowered in central Anatolia (Turkey) between the 19th and 13th centuries B.C. Hittites were Caucasoid Indo-European-speaking invaders, ruling as feudal aristocrats from their capital Hattusas (excavated near the present-day village of Boghazkoy). Hittites pioneered iron weapons, rode war chariots pulled by horses, worshiped many deities, and had an arable and pastoral economy, and a remarkably humane law code.

After the empire collapsed its cultural traditions continued to thrive in provincial cities for another seven centuries, when the last Hittite states were absorbed by the Assyrian Empire.

HYPOCAUST A hollow space beneath a floor, carrying heated air from a furnace and so warming a house or a bath. It was a common form of central heating used by the Romans.

ICE AGE A period in earth history when ice covered more of the earth than it does now. The last great glaciation comprised four major periods of advancing ice—named the Günz, Mindel, Riss, and Würm periods. The Günz began over 600,000 years ago. The Würm ended about 12,000 years ago. Each period was punctuated by temporary retreats of the ice and a mild interglacial period (the longest lasting 190,000 years) separated each period from the next. At its greatest extent, in the Mindel glaciation, an ice sheet covered much of Europe, Asia, and North America.

INCAS South American Indians centered in the Peruvian Andes. Between A.D. 950 and 1500 they built and despotically ruled an empire of eight million subjects—many living in cities linked by 10,000 miles of road.

Inca culture was based on earlier Peruvian civilizations. It featured agriculture, coastal navigation, advanced engineering, architecture, textiles, ceramics, music, poetry, and fine gold work. Yet it lacked the use of wheels, plows, writing, and—to any extent—metal tools. In 1536 a handful of Spanish troops easily took control of the empire from its Inca rulers.

View of an Iron-Age hill-fort

Hittite war chariot

Inca warrior

Tomb of Kings   *The Valley of the Kings (top) concealed the tombs of about 30 Egyptian pharaohs. The most magnificent was that of Tutankhamen, which held, among other treasures, a throne decorated with portraits of the king and his queen.*

INDUSTRIAL ARCHAEOLOGY Archaeology concerned with the industrial revolution of the 18th and 19th centuries—for instance early cotton mills, iron-framed buildings, shipyards, and blast furnaces.

INDUS VALLEY CIVILIZATION One of the world's first civilizations. Developed by dark-skinned Dravidian peoples, it flourished about 2500 B.C. in over 40 Indus Valley towns and villages—notably in two major centers, Mohenjo-Daro and Harappa. The culture included standard weights, cotton growing and weaving, domesticated elephants, ox-carts, bronze tools, city drainage, and trading connections with Sumer. Indo-European Aryans from central Asia crushed the civilization soon after 2000 B.C.

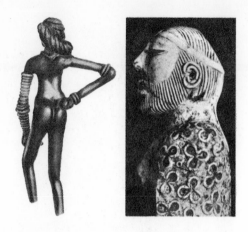

Examples of Indus Valley art

INSCRIPTIONS Words written on a monument, coin, document, etc. They may be inscribed in ink on paper or cut in stone, metal, or wood.

IRON AGE The period in cultural evolution that followed the Bronze Age☞. It began about 1500 B.C. in west Asia.

JERICHO The site (in Jordan) of the world's oldest known town, eight acres in area, founded over 9000 years ago near a perennial spring.

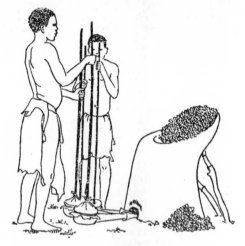

Primitive iron-smelting

KNOSSOS Site of a major Minoan city in Crete☞, remarkable for an elaborate palace that, about 2000 B.C., apparently served as a religious and administrative center. About 1400 B.C. the palace was destroyed, and the city eventually abandoned.

LA VENTA (OR OLMEC) A pre-Columbian culture that emerged in the Valley of Mexico and spread south to El Salvador—possibly the first of all American civilizations, dated by radio-carbon to 1500 B.C. and reaching its highest point about 1000-500 B.C.

La Venta people had a calendar system (possibly the origin of the Mayas'), probably developed monumental pyramids at Teotihuacan☞, and carved remarkable monolithic basalt heads, delicate jade statuettes, and finely drilled beads. La Venta sculpture suggests an obsession with human deformity and a cult of jaguar worship.

La Venta statue

Fire-making in the Old Stone Age

Mayan statue from Copan

LEVALLOISIAN A Paleolithic☞ culture featuring the use of fire and of stone tools made from especially prepared cores. Flakes struck from such cores automatically became blade tools with no need for retouching.

This tool-making technique—possibly derived from Acheulian☞ and Clactonian☞ technology—flourished in Africa and northwest Europe from about 250,000 to 75,000 years ago.

LOWER PALEOLITHIC See PALEOLITHIC.

LYNCHET A bank formed at the bottom of a sloping field by loosened soil creeping down furrows produced by plowing. In southern England, lynchets reveal cultivation dating from the Late Bronze Age☞ to Roman times.

MAGDALENIAN The last of three major Upper Paleolithic☞ cultures in western Europe, featuring reindeer-hunting and tools including unretouched stone blades, also awls, needles, etc. of bone and antler. See also AURIGNACIAN and SOLUTREAN.

MAORIS Polynesian inhabitants of New Zealand. When discovered by the English explorer Captain Cook in 1769, they had a Neolithic☞ culture. The Maoris had settled New Zealand between A.D. 900-1400, sailing and paddling canoes from Tahiti (1600 miles away).

MASADA Hilltop site of the palace fortress of Herod the Great—ruler of Palestine in the last third of the first century B.C. One thousand Jewish nationalists defied the Romans there in A.D. 73 before committing suicide rather than submit.

MAYAPAN The last great Mayan city, destroyed by war in the 15th century A.D.

MAYAS Indians who built one of the world's great civilizations, in pre-Columbian Middle America (notably in the Yucatan peninsula). By the time it reached its peak, about A.D. 1000, the Mayas had developed shifting agriculture, ceremonial cities with stone pyramids capped by temples, astronomical observatories, systems of pictographic writing, mathematics employing a sign for zero, and an accurate calendar. But

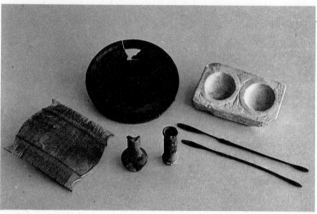

Fortress of Death

The rock fortress of Masada was the scene of a mass suicide in A.D. 73, when 960 Jewish Zealots took their lives there rather than surrender to the Romans. Discoveries made on the site in the years 1953-55 included a basket that held a Roman army paymaster's quittance roll (upper left), a comb, a mirror, and other cosmetic utensils (left), earthenware oil lamps, storage jars, and mosaics.

Darius I, King of Media and Persia

Megalith at Carnac, France

they lacked metal tools, the wheel, and the plow. Toltec☞ invaders from the north took over their culture about A.D. 1000.

MEDES Indo-European-speaking peoples of the Iranian group who settled the great plateau between the Caspian Sea and the Persian Gulf. In 559 B.C. they joined forces with their Iranian neighbors, the Persians. The combined groups developed first a kingdom, then the colossal Achaemenid Empire. See also PERSIA.

MEGALITH From the Greek for "big stone." It describes the monumental standing stones☞, stone circles, and graves☞ built in Neolithic☞ and Bronze Age☞ times in coastal areas from the East Mediterranean to the Baltic Sea, suggestive of contacts between peoples living in those areas. Megalithic tombs also occur in south and southeast Asia.

MESOLITHIC Of the Middle Stone Age (from the Greek for "middle" and "stone")—a stone-using hunting group of cultures, placed between the Paleolithic☞ and Neolithic☞ Ages, whose characteristic tools included axes, traps, boats, and composite hunting implements containing microliths☞.

Its development coincided with the retreat of glaciers at the close of the last Ice Age☞ and largely represents a response to changing environmental conditions (such as the growth of forests). Mesolithic cultures in west Asia began giving way to Neolithic cultures by 9000 years ago. In Australia and Southwest Africa, Bushmen and Aborigines still practice largely Mesolithic ways of life.

MICROLITH A type of tiny flint tool, often geometrically shaped, used chiefly by Mesolithic☞ peoples. By fitting rows of microlithic blades into shafts of bone or wood they produced harpoons and other composite tools.

MIDDLE STONE AGE See MESOLITHIC.

MIGRATIONS Movements from place to place—notably intercontinental migrations by which the Americas and Australia were peopled by Paleolithic☞ groups (assisted by the low sea levels that then prevailed), and subsequent large-scale movements (for instance in Polynesia and Micronesia) facilitated by the development of boats.

Archaeologists infer migration from geographical comparison of race, language, and other evidence provided by extinct and living cultures☞.

MINOAN CIVILIZATION The Bronze-Age☞ civilization of Crete☞.

MIXTECS Indians inhabiting the state of Oaxaca, Mexico, in pre-Columbian times. They built great stone tombs, produced intricate gold ornaments, and spread the worship of Quetzalcoatl, the feathered serpent.

Mixtec pendant

MOHENJO-DARO One of two major cities established by the Indus Valley civilization☞ in what is now West Pakistan.

MONTE ALBAN Mountain-top site 300 miles south of Mexico City of a ceremonial pre-Columbian city begun A.D. 1000. The site occupies 25 square miles and contains remarkable temples, tombs, altars and works of art.

Archaeologists believe the city passed through seven epochs bearing the successive stamp of La Venta☞, Mayan☞, and other cultures.

MOSAIC A pattern made up from many tiny pieces of colored stone, glass, or shell. Since Sumerian times—about 5000 years ago—craftsmen have used mosaic patterns and pictures to decorate surfaces ranging from a checkerboard to a floor.

MOUSTERIAN The Paleolithic☞ culture produced by Neanderthal man☞ and characterized by skillfully retouched core☞ and flake tools☞, wooden spears, the use of fire, cave-dwelling, burial of the dead, and cannibalism. It is named for finds in rock shelters at Le Moustier, France, but the culture flourished from western Europe to Palestine, between about 70,000 and 20,000 years ago.

MUMMY A dead body that has been preserved— naturally, as with pre-Columbian mummies in Peru (preserved by the dry climate), or by

Egyptian mummy

Neanderthal man

deliberately embalming, as with Egyptian pharaohs☞ (whose bodies were soaked for months in a preservative alkaline solution).

MUSEUM A building for storing and displaying objects of interest. Museums date from at least 550 B.C. (at Ur☞). But private collectors began grouping objects systematically only during the Renaissance, and public museums remained almost unknown until the 19th century.

NEANDERTHAL MAN An extinct species of man with protruding brows and receding chin who flourished in Europe and west Asia between 70,000 and 20,000 years ago. His Mousterian☞ culture equipped him to hunt the mammoth and rhinoceros and to adapt himself to a cold climate.

NEOLITHIC Of the New Stone Age (from the Greek for "new" and "stone")—the period in cultural evolution between the Mesolithic☞ and Bronze Ages☞, named for its fine stone tools, polished by grinding. However, the main criterion for distinguishing Neolithic from Paleolithic☞ cultures is Neolithic man's ability to produce food by agriculture or stock raising instead of by hunting and foraging.

Neolithic societies arose—apparently independently—in Asia perhaps 12,000 years ago, in the Americas about 9000 years ago. In each continent farming produced a food surplus supporting enlarged populations, permanent villages, and social cooperation—the basis of civilization.

NEW STONE AGE See NEOLITHIC.

Statue of a winged bull from Nimrud

NIMRUD An ancient Assyrian city near the Tigris River in what is now Iraq. Austen Layard excavated the city in the mid-19th century.

NINEVEH An ancient city on the east bank of the Tigris River in what is now Iraq. As the capital of the Assyrian Empire (see ASSYRIANS) Nineveh housed a remarkable library of clay tablets drawn from all parts of the empire. The city was destroyed about 612 B.C. by Medes☞ and Babylonians. Its remains were excavated by Austen Layard in the mid-19th century.

OBELISK A tapering monolithic column with a square base and pyramidal top. The ancient Egyptians placed obelisks in pairs as monuments at temple entrances. The shadows cast by obelisks helped their astronomers to determine what we term the points of the compass.

OLDOWAN AND KAFUAN Cultures comprising the oldest known tools—pebbles flaked at one or more edges, sometimes into a point, and probably used for cutting, chopping, or scraping. Pebble tools are associated with the remains of so-called Handy Man (*Homo habilis*), Nutcracker Man (*Zinjanthropus boisei*), and other Australopithecine fossils of east and south Africa.

OLD STONE AGE See PALEOLITHIC.

OLMECS See LA VENTA.

PALENQUE A Mayan religious center in Chiapas state, Mexico, dating from about A.D. 300. Its buildings include temples, steam baths, a road, and an aqueduct that is still in use.

PALEOLITHIC Of the Old Stone Age (from the Greek for "old" and "stone")—a period in cultural evolution that lasted about two million years and is subdivided into Lower, Middle, and Upper Paleolithic.

The Lower Paleolithic (from about two million to 100,000 years ago) comprises the Oldowan☞, Choukoutien☞, Abbevillian☞, Acheulian☞, Clactonian☞, and other primarily food-gathering cultures☞ based on simple stone core☞ or flake tools☞.

Middle Paleolithic describes Mousterian☞ culture, not a chronological period.

Upper Paleolithic (about 100,000 to 14,000 years ago) includes the Aurignacian☞, Solutrean☞, Magdalenian☞, and other hunting cultures involving stone blades and a variety of bone and wooden tools. See also MESOLITHIC and NEOLITHIC.

PAPYRUS A tall reed-like water plant used as writing material by the ancient Egyptians. They cut its pith in strips, pressed them into a sheet cemented by juices, then dried and polished the sheet to produce a smooth surface.

Tool-making in the Stone Age

Part of a papyrus document

The Legendary King   *King Arthur, if he ever existed outside medieval legend, may have been a sixth-century Romano-British chief. Photographs show excavations at Glastonbury Tor (top), perhaps his burial place, and at South Cadbury, a possible Camelot.*

PARTHENON A famous Greek temple whose remains crown the Acropolis☞ at Athens. It was built in the fifth century B.C. and dedicated to Athene, goddess of wisdom.

PEAT Decayed compacted plant remains that form in marshy places. Archaeologists use pollen samples from borings made in peat bogs to date and identify prehistoric vegetation. See POLLEN ANALYSIS.

PERSIA A nation founded in 559 B.C. by the Iranian tribes called Medes☞ and Persians. By 480 B.C. the Achaemenid dynasty of Persian rulers had enlarged it into an empire stretching from India to Greece. It was captured by Alexander the Great (331 B.C.), fought for by Rome, resurrected by the Persian Sassanid dynasty (A.D. 226-651), then under the successive Moslem rule of Arabs, Turks, and Mongols. Modern Persia (Iran) dates from the rise of a new Persian dynasty about A.D. 1500.

Median and Persian soldiers

PHARAOH From "Per-aah," the Egyptian for "Great house"—the name given to the hereditary kings (and supposed gods) who ruled ancient Egypt from about 3000 B.C. to the sixth century B.C. when Persian invaders overthrew them.

PHOENICIANS Semitic peoples formerly inhabiting what is now Lebanon, on the east Mediterranean coast. Using a plentiful timber supply to build sea-going ships, they wove a network of Mediterranean trade routes and—after the 12th century B.C.—set up colonies as far west as Spain. Their chief cultural contribution was the development of an alphabet that gave rise to our own.

POLLEN ANALYSIS Discovering the kinds of plants that lived in past ages by studying the remains of their pollen in the soil. By counting all the pollen grains in a given piece of soil, experts can show just which plants were rare and which were plentiful. Counts taken at different soil levels show how the pattern of vegetation varied as climates and methods of land use changed.

POTTERY Containers dating from Neolithic☞ (and sometimes Mesolithic☞) times onward, made from baked clay and originally shaped by

The pharaoh Rameses II

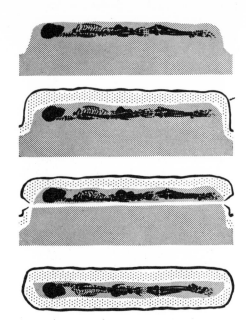

How soil holding a skeleton may be cut out in a solid block and sealed

building up clay "worms," but, from about 3250 B.C. in west Asia, molded on a wheel.

Local impurities in clay, variations in pottery shapes, decorations, and methods of firing all help archaeologists to plot the development, diffusion, and decline of prehistoric cultures☞.

PREHISTORIC MAN Men of our own and other, now extinct, species living in prehistoric times. See EARLY MAN, PALEOLITHIC, MESOLITHIC, and NEOLITHIC.

PREHISTORY The period in man's cultural development before history began. History may be said to date from the first written records (about 5500 years ago in west Asia).

PRESERVATION In archaeology, protecting evidence of the past from damage or decay—for instance coating fragile skeletons in wax to prevent damage during excavation, and steeping objects in liquid polyvinyl acetate to produce a surface layer that keeps out air and so prevents decay or rusting.

PYRAMID A type of stone or brick monument with a square base and sloping sides, built by ancient Egyptians as a royal tomb, by civilizations of pre-Columbian Middle America as a raised platform for temples.

The tallest pyramid is the Egyptian royal tomb of the Pharaoh Khufu, about 480 feet high, and raised more than 4500 years ago. The biggest in volume is the pre-Columbian Cholula pyramid near Puebla, Mexico (containing 4,300,000 cubic yards of stone against 3,360,000 in the Khufu pyramid).

RADIOACTIVITY The emission of particles from the nuclei of certain atoms. Radioactive elements lose their radioactivity at a steady rate. By measuring its radioactive content with a Geiger counter☞ scientists can often tell the age of a given element.

RECONSTRUCTION Rebuilding damaged or missing objects as closely as possible to their originals. For instance, by pouring wax into the space left by a totally decayed object buried in soil, an archaeologist can reconstruct its shape.

Egyptian pyramid

Reconstructing a decayed object's substance is also possible after chemical analysis of the stains it has left behind in the soil.

RESISTIVITY SURVEYING Discovering buried objects by inserting electrodes in the soil and passing a current between them. The voltage varies with the moisture in the soil, which in turn depends upon the substances that the soil contains. By recording voltage variations over a given area, a surveyor can pinpoint sites worth excavating.

SCROLL A roll of parchment or similar flexible material that in Egypt and parts of west Asia served the purpose of a book before the invention of books made from bound sheets.

The use of parchment scrolls dates from a second-century B.C. Egyptian prohibition on the export of papyrus☞ to Asia Minor. As a substitute for papyrus, the citizens of Pergamum learned to split, scrape, and prepare animal skins as a writing material.

SIDON An ancient Phoenician☞ city-state and its city—a rich port on the east Mediterranean coast. Merchants built up the city's wealth by trading with lands as far west as Spain.

SOLUTREAN An Upper Paleolithic☞ culture that flourished in France and central Europe after the Aurignacian☞ culture. Its artefacts☞ include long, pressure-flaked, bifacial blade tools, and show that the Solutreans hunted mammoths.

SPECTROGRAPHIC ANALYSIS A method of discovering the composition of a substance by analyzing the light that it emits when heated. In X-ray spectrographic analysis, a beam of X rays passing through a metal projects a pattern on a photographic plate. The pattern is formed by the atoms making up the metal. At a given temperature, each metal produces its own characteristic pattern. Thus X-ray spectrographic analysis helps archaeologists to determine the metal or metals in an unidentified substance.

SPHINX A figure with the body of a lion and the head of a man or animal—a characteristic sculptural form in ancient Egypt. The most

The Great Sphinx at Giza

famous of all sphinxes—the Great Sphinx at Giza—is 240 feet long and 66 feet high; it was cut out of a solid knoll of rock over 4500 years ago. Its original purpose remains obscure, but the Egyptians possibly venerated it as the embodiment of a sun god.

STANDING STONE   Stone monoliths (also termed menhirs) raised in western Europe in Bronze-Age☞ times. They occur singly, in circles, and in rows—notably at Carnac, Brittany, where thousands of menhirs up to 13 feet high are aligned in over 30 parallel rows—some of them more than 1000 yards long.

STELE   An upright pillar or slab, often carved and inscribed, and—especially in classical Greece—used as a gravestone. Archaeologically significant examples include a Babylonian stone shaft engraved with a copy of the so-called Code of Hammurabi (one of the oldest known law codes) and the so-called calendar stones of the Mayas☞.

STONE AGE   The period when stone was the hardest substance with which man was able to make tools. It began about two million years ago and still persists in remote parts of southwest Africa, South America, and Australia.

The Stone Age is divided into the Paleolithic☞, Mesolithic☞, and Neolithic☞ ages.

STONEHENGE   Best-known ancient monument in the British Isles, begun by Neolithic☞ peoples about 1900 B.C. as a sacred area marked by a 300-feet-diameter circle of pits flanked by a bank and ditch. By 1400 B.C. additions included an outer banked avenue, and concentrically inside the circle of pits two more pit circles and a post-and-lintel arrangement of giant stones weighing over 45 tons each. Some probably took more than 550 men to place them in position, using ropes and earth ramps. Stonehenge was used for religious rituals and some of its stone alignments suggest that these had associations with astronomical events.

SUMERIANS   Bronze-Age peoples of unidentified west Asian origin and type who introduced writing and metallurgy to Mesopotamia. By

Stele of the Code of Hammurabi

5500 years ago they were developing the world's first civilization with city states ruled by the "tenant farmers" of city gods. They had copper and—soon afterwards—bronze tools and weapons, agriculture based on irrigation, systems of weights and measures, law codes, writing, the wheel, and monumental brick-built ziggurats☞. Sumerian power ultimately declined under attacks from neighboring peoples, but Sumerian culture was eventually transmitted to Europe and is largely the basis of modern civilization.

TEOTIHUACAN Literally "Home of the Gods"—the Mexican site of a pre-Columbian city remarkable for its massive pyramids, notably the Pyramid of the Sun: 216 feet high, containing 55,000 cubic yards of stone weighing three million tons, it was built about 900 B.C., possibly by the La Venta☞ people.

Reconstruction of Pyramid of the Sun

TERRACOTTA A fine clay that has been molded and baked and is always reddish in color.

In ancient Greece and Italy, terracotta was widely used for decorative roof tiles and for statuettes to be placed in tombs. In Italy, the traditional craftsmanship associated with making terracotta objects still survives.

TOLTECS Literally "Master Builders"—Nahau-speaking Indians possibly originating in Guatemala who (about A.D. 650) established a short-lived empire in the Valley of Mexico.

Building on the earlier achievements of other Middle American Indians, they became great architects, astronomers, artists, and craftsmen and their farmers grew maize, cotton, chili peppers, beans, and all other domesticated plants then known in Mexico, while Toltec rulers established a system of tax-collection followed eventually by the Aztecs☞.

About A.D. 950 the empire collapsed in civil war, and the succeeding famines and epidemics temporarily checked cultural development in Middle America.

But before this happened, emigrant Toltecs had enlarged Mayan cities with impressive stone and mortar buildings adorned by ornate sculptures and fine murals.

Like other pre-Columbian civilizations, they lacked the wheel, the plow, and metal tools.

Toltec warriors

Rein ring found at Ur

How cuneiform writing began

Assyrian scribe

TYRE A modern port in Lebanon on the east coast of the Mediterranean, formerly one of the chief Phoenician city-states. It established trading settlements—notably at Carthage☞—on the North African, Spanish, and Sicilian coasts as early as 1200 B.C.

UPPER PALEOLITHIC See PALEOLITHIC.

UR The site, in what is now Iraq, of a remarkable brick-built Sumerian☞ city that flourished as early as 3000 B.C. It featured defensive walls, temples, a ziggurat☞, and richly furnished royal burials testifying to a high level of culture.

VALLEY OF THE KINGS West of the Nile near Luxor. Starting with Tuthmosis I (about 1515 B.C.) it became a cemetery for pharaohs whose tombs were cut into the rock sides of the valley.

VILLA Type of Roman residence comprising a range of rooms linked by a corridor or veranda, often built around a courtyard. Luxurious villas had mosaic☞ floors and baths, and many had hypocausts☞.

WRITING Representing objects and ideas by ideographic signs (visually related to them) or phonetic signs (related to the sounds of the words for them). Systems of writing developed in west Asia about 3500 B.C., in east Asia by 1500 B.C., and in Middle America by 800 B.C.

ZAPOTEC Literally "Eaters of Zapote Fruit"—Indians inhabiting part of pre-Columbian Mexico who developed a rich civilization in what is now the state of Daxaca and ruled Monte Alban☞ about A.D. 600.

ZIGGURAT A type of brick-built stepped pyramid, crowned by a temple dedicated to a local god, and common to all major Sumerian cities.

The fully excavated ziggurat at Ur☞ consisted of a mass of sun-dried bricks faced with kiln-fired bricks set in bitumen, its base about 200 by 150 feet, its summit 70 feet high reached by outer stairways that climbed its receding terraces. Besides conducting religious ceremonies from its summit, priests made astronomical observations there.

Index

Picture Credits

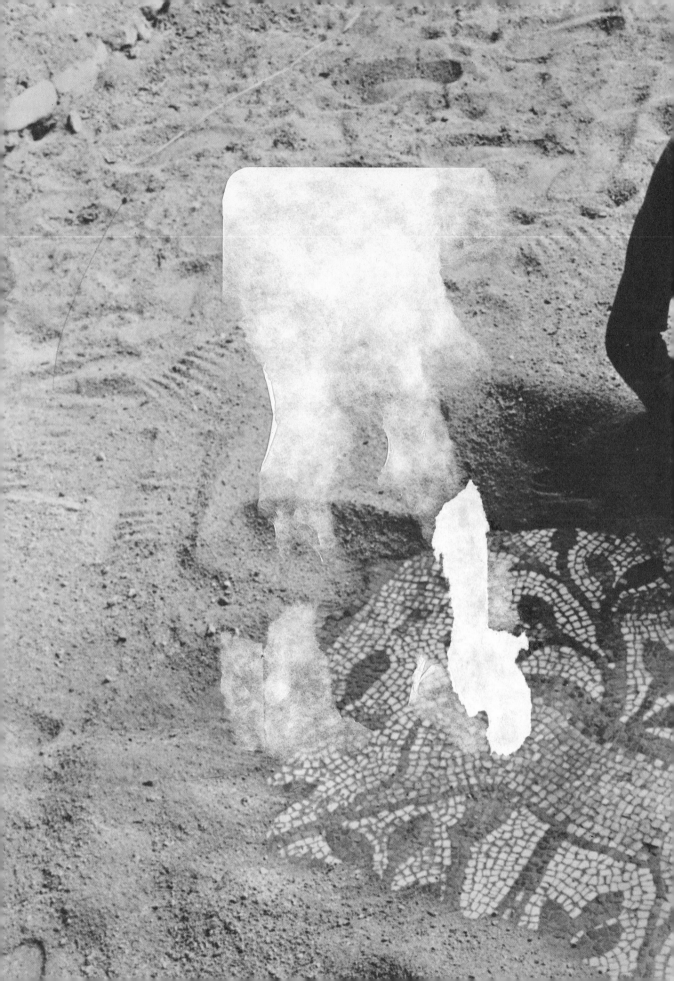